SMALL BUSINESS

362.61
FER   Ferry, James.

           How to start a
           home-based senior
           care business

how to sta

Senior

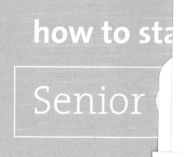

ebster

Public Library
Webster, NY 14580
872-7075

how to start a home-based

Senior Care Business

James L. Ferry

Guilford, Connecticut

Copyright © 2010 by Morris Book Publishing, LLC

Text designed by Sheryl P. Kober

Library of Congress Cataloging-in-Publication Data is available on file.

ISBN 978-0-7627-5013-9

Printed in the United States of America
10 9 8 7 6 5 4 3 2 1

I would like to dedicate this book to my youngest brother, Brendan John Ferry, who was a careful thinker, gifted musician, and caring person.

You, who left us too soon, and I miss you—*cronaím thú.*

Contents

Acknowledgments

I would first like to thank my professional colleagues in social work, health care, and geriatric care management. Much of what I know about professional human service and business is the result of what we have talked about and experienced together.

But most important, I would like to acknowledge the support that I am continuously granted from my wife, Dr. Margaret Anne Ferry, loving wife, nurturing mother, and inspiring physician.

Introduction

The completion of *How to Start a Home-Based Senior Care Business* has coincided with a national debate on health care reform in the United States. Many in this debate feel strongly that the finest aspects of health care delivery in America are represented in innovative products and services originating from entrepreneurship. It is my contention that innovative service-based businesses will increasingly be developed to meet the needs of the burgeoning numbers of seniors.

Successful senior care entrepreneurs tend to be caring, imaginative people from an eclectic array of professional backgrounds. They are simultaneously able to understand the needs of seniors and then create business models that serve as solutions to problems that are commonly experienced by older and disabled adults. Aspiring senior care entrepreneurs should expect that there will be a considerable amount of learning involved along the way. Some of these entrepreneurs come from professional backgrounds in health or human services and thus encounter a steep learning curve related to business planning, development, and marketing. Others are from business backgrounds and have to initially understand the lives and needs of seniors and the senior care marketplace before devising a successful senior care business model.

Successful senior care entrepreneurs need to possess and convey an attitude of caring while also being serious and responsible about business. Senior care is not an area for opportunistic serial entrepreneurs who have no interest in the field of aging. A lack of genuine interest in the elderly population will likely be perceived by people in the marketplace and will prevent success. Likewise, aspiring senior care entrepreneurs who have always been an employee in a health or human service organization sector will need to learn as much as they can about the realities of owning their own businesses before "quitting their day jobs." A long time ago an experienced entrepreneur advised me that "being in business for yourself means you work a lot more and earn lot more." This advice has turned out to be true for me.

I hope this book gives you the inspiration and the necessary information and perspective for starting your senior care business. While it contains what is expected and essential in a book about start-up businesses, I have also included my particular perspective as a veteran home-based senior care entrepreneur. There will inevitably be additional written resources that you will need to access for your business start-up. I have suggested some resources in this volume. If you have already begun your reading of small business entrepreneurial books (and you should read several!), I am honored that you have chosen *How to Start a Home-Based Senior Care Business* as part of your startup entrepreneur's library.

Best wishes on your future endeavor!

—Jim Ferry

So You Want to Start Your Own Senior Care Business

There is no question that the fields of aging are growing as the population of older adults in the United States and in many other nations increases. The central reason for this increase in the aging population has to do with advances in health care in the areas of disease prevention and management. Fifty years ago, the average life expectancy was 67.55 years of age. In 2009, the average life expectancy was 75 years of age. There is every indication that this trend will continue.

Does the fact that people are living longer mean that they are living better? Not necessarily. Many older adults contend with an array of chronic health, and sometimes mental health, conditions. As a result, older adults often manage with difficulty in their own homes or in retirement housing, having either no relatives or relatives who live far away. Elders who are more frail often end up in assisted living facilities (ALF) or skilled nursing facilities (SNF), but may experience care that is inadequate or of poor quality. These older adults with some measure of frailty may require new, different, or improved services in order to have optimally healthy and functional lives.

It is the role of senior care professionals to serve elderly people in need of specialized services in order to live as comfortably and as independently as possible. These specialized services can fall into an array of service areas, including but not limited to home care, geriatric care management, aging-related individual and family psychotherapy, private rehabilitation and exercise therapy, chore service, bill paying and medical billing advocacy, professional organizing, move managing, or personal chef services.

Turn Personal Experience into a Business

Senior care business owners come from an array of professional backgrounds and academic preparation, such as social work, nursing, education,

In 1994 there were approximately 500 members of the National Association of Professional Geriatric Managers. Currently that number has quadrupled to over 2,000. Nearly all GCMs in practice report year-to-year growth, and there is no reason to expect less in the coming years.

counseling, rehabilitation therapy, and business management. Aspiring senior care business owners are motivated by an opportunity to build an organization (even a small one-person organization, at least to start) in an industry that will likely expand despite a current serious downturn in the economies of the United States and many other countries. Some senior care business owners report being inspired to serve elders after having a meaningful experience in caring for an elderly relative. Senior care business owners with a professional background in health or human services may have become "burned out" after years of working in agency or facility settings and are now excited by the prospect of starting, owning, and operating a senior care business of their making.

It is imperative that an aspiring senior care business owner have a personal passion for wanting to make a positive difference in the lives of elders. It is also necessary that elder care professionals have a "thick skin" for dealing with people—including elderly clients, family members, friends, and other professionals—with difficult realities and difficult choices to make. Successful elder care professionals often need to assess and synthesize information about the health and mental health issues of their clients. Additionally, they are often expected to know about resources and services available to the aging population. Successful elder care professionals also possess an ability to be compassionate and empathetic, and also to be up front and direct when this becomes necessary in order to help their clients.

Many home-based senior care professionals begin their careers as solo practitioners or business owners. One important feature of serving frail elders is that clients often find it difficult to travel and prefer to be visited at home. A traditional office is thus often unnecessary, particularly if the new senior care business owner has access to private meeting spaces on an intermittent basis. Experienced senior care business owners will tell you that they live by an up-to-date computer, an office phone, and an automobile that is presentable and reliable. Additional up-front investments include marketing and advertising materials, software for billing and information management, and fees for conferences, associations, and professional organizations.

The Income Realities of a Startup Entrepreneur

A major challenge for the aspiring senior care entrepreneur is being able to afford your current lifestyle while you plan and execute the numerous tasks that are necessary before you serve that first client. You will need financial resources to live on while you work in the startup phase of your business. Additionally, you will need to invest financial resources in order to get your business established. "Don't quit your day job" is likely sound advice for the aspiring senior care entrepreneur, assuming you have a job that you can keep. It may, however, be difficult to deal with startup tasks, including marketing calls, if your current job requires you to work typical Monday through Friday business hours. Some emerging entrepreneurs are able to live reasonably off their savings for a period of time in order to work on the establishment of their businesses.

If you are unable to leave your current employment in order to focus on building your senior care business on a full-time basis, consider the following approaches in order to support yourself and your family while building your business:

- Change the hours of your current job to allow you to engage in some business startup activities during traditional business hours (9:00 a.m. to 5:00 p.m.).
- Create time for your startup by reducing the total weekly hours you work, provided that you can afford it and that you won't lose any health care benefits.
- Consider leaving your current position for a new job (possibly in the elder care field) with fewer hours, or with night or weekend hours. This will allow for weekday hours for marketing and networking your startup business.
- Secure an available credit line and very carefully use these funds to live on for a very short time. You should, however, consult with your accountant, who might regard this as a risky approach in terms of the future solvency of your startup business.

If you are currently employed in the field of elder care, or if you make the pragmatic decision to work for a senior care oriented company or agency, you may not be allowed to market your startup senior care business to other employees or clients of that entity. Reputation is everything in the human service fields (as it is in other fields), so cultivating a reputation as a businessperson of high integrity, honesty, and professionalism will be vital for enduring success.

What It Means to Be Self-Employed

Self-employment will inevitably mean a change in lifestyle. As an entrepreneur in any business, you will typically work longer hours than you had when you were someone's employee, and the areas about which you need to be informed and tasks to be taken on are far more varied than in other positions you may have previously held. Having said this, it is also widely known that entrepreneurs typically earn more money year to year than employees. Additionally, and perhaps quite poignantly given the current economic downturn, there is an obvious level of job security in owning your own business as opposed to working for an employer where even a solid employee might be laid off, even arbitrarily.

Of course, job security as an entrepreneur is dependent on the financial health and overall success of the business. That is, does the business attract paying customers? Owners of senior care businesses report that there is often a wide and increasing need for the services that they provide. They will also caution that a client's ability to pay depends on the elder or family member's financial position. Senior care businesses that accept third-party payments for service (most typically from government or commercial medical or long-term care insurance policies) may have a more predictable stream of income, but have other challenges around receiving payments.

Overall, it is probably fair to say that entrepreneurs face more varied challenges and work harder than employees, yet successful entrepreneurs enjoy greater job security and earn more money.

The Business Mindset Versus the Agency Mindset

Some aspiring senior care entrepreneurs come from the business world, where to some extent they work predictable hours with relatively understood job duties. Other aspiring senior care entrepreneurs are health care or human service professionals with relatively extensive experience working for agencies or health facilities. In these settings, these professionals typically focus on clinically oriented duties while administrative or policy-oriented tasks are the purview of administrators. A professional staff member with prescribed duties for a set number of hours per week may be employed by a facility or agency that has responsibility for and a capacity to serve clients (or patients) around the clock via an array of personnel working shifts.

Dealing with That "On-Call" Issue

In contrast to traditional employment, owning and growing a home-based senior care business will usher in work and lifestyle changes for entrepreneurs from either business or health and human service backgrounds. For some, providing services to an aging consumer, often with problems or needs beyond the Monday through Friday 9:00 a.m. to 5:00 p.m. time frame, will mean a significant lifestyle adjustment. While an aspiring entrepreneur may feel weary of commuting to a job and may hold a romanticized view of working at home, many home-based entrepreneurs report regret at the loss of the boundary between "work" and "home."

Most entrepreneurs earning a living will speak to the sometimes daunting nature of full-time self-employment. After years of working for an organization, the notion that receiving a paycheck as an entrepreneur is directly tied to consistently bringing in business through serving clients and receiving payments is likely to produce some level of anxiety, especially early on. Entrepreneurs live with the reality that there is never a guarantee of a paycheck and that almost always, everyone else needs to be paid before you. Additionally, entrepreneurs can feel downright intimidated by the lack of predictability in so many areas of service-based small business ownership. A full-time geriatric care manager in private practice once commented to me, "I really enjoy waking up each morning not knowing what the new work day will bring!" I remember at the time reflecting on her statement, thinking that prospect did not sound particularly appealing to me.

Entrepreneurship "done right" requires tenacity and resilience. At times it means servicing clients at the expense of leisure and time with family and friends. Entrepreneurship involving service to clients in need requires a new orientation toward your work where to some extent you are always "on call" and in the roles of practitioner, marketer, and manager.

Elevator Speech for a Highly Personalized Business

Before you decide on a name for your business, buy office furniture, or order stationery, it's vital first to dream generally, and then to conceptualize more specifically what you want to do in your business. Then you're ready to set out to plan your business carefully. Dream about the positive aims you have for your business and how you will help aging clients in need, but don't forget to consider the potential for abundance in terms of personal and professional satisfaction and hopefully income, and how this might positively change the lifestyle of your family and yourself.

Consider the options of what you could do in your home-based senior care business, and then try out each idea in the form of "elevator speech."

Resources for the Exploratory Phase

Family Members or Friends

As you begin the exploratory phase, you'll want to inventory your resources. Think about the people that you are close to. Do they have the time, interest, and expertise to help your startup business? Think about current friends and perhaps old friends. Additionally, make sure that you are fully acquainted with the experience and expertise of family members, including extended family. Consider whether people in your personal life might be sources of advice, counsel, or valuable contacts for business development or for marketing your business. Completing a networking form, such as the "Team 100" developed by Thomas Leonard (www.coachville.com/basic/team100/sampleissue.html), can be a very valuable exercise for identifying the people with whom you interface regularly in your day-to-day life. Introducing your business at the startup phase to professionals in your community with whom you are aligned, such as your dentist, banker, accountant, or car mechanic, may very likely result in someone providing invaluable help to you in terms of business development and marketing.

Successful Senior Care Professionals

Allied professionals, most likely in the health or aging fields, are often very willing to be helpful to aspiring entrepreneurs who are also interested in helping others. Professionals who are proud of and enjoy what they do are often quite willing to lend their time. This is particularly true if the future small business could be considered complementary to the aims of that professional's organization, as opposed to competitive. With this in mind, consider the vital task of informational interviewing of these professionals. Invite them to lunch, and of course insist on paying! Expect the outcome of some of these meetings to be invaluable "inside track" information that you might never otherwise know.

Professional Organizations

If you already belong to a professional organization or are eligible to belong to one, consider the potential of the organization to promote you and your business through a directory of members that they publish either in print or online. You may never have thought of an organization germane to your profession as a marketing tool, but as you explore their Web sites this potential may become apparent. It is important to note that success in many areas of elder services is contingent on a long-distance relative or friend being aware of a particular senior care business. This is due to the fact that elders who live at a distance from close family and friends are typically the ones most in need of services. Many, if not all, professions and business categories have organizations, including the National Association of Social Workers, National Association of Home Care and Hospice, and the National Gerontological Nursing Association.

An example of an important organization pertaining to senior care is the National Association of Professional Geriatric Care Managers (NAPGCM; www .caremanager.org). NAPGCM is an organization of professionals in the field of care management. Geriatric care managers (GCMs) are health or human services professionals who assist family members or others in caring for elders. GCMs come to care management from various fields related to long-term care, including nursing, gerontology, social work, or psychology. Through a fund of knowledge and specialized skills, a GCM helps elders with attaining their optimal function, typically through assessment and then identification and provision of services. A GCM also assists family members, friends, or involved professionals by serving as a willing expert and coach. GCMs often work in individual practices (often home-based) or in small group practices, and typically serve clients who live near to them.

As is the case for other senior care businesses, GCMs are often not contracted by the elders themselves and are instead hired by a long-distance family member or friend. Through an online and printed directory, NAPGCM offers potential clients well-delineated information regarding member GCMs. Additionally, membership in

NAPGCM includes an "Affiliate" category, which includes members not in the direct practice of care management but with an interest in the aging field, such as attorneys, medical professionals, and individuals representing home health agencies, nursing homes, assisted living facilities, and so on.

Specialization

One consideration for a home-based senior care entrepreneur is whether to specialize or to develop a niche client population. This question is often asked by senior care professionals who are working in a community where there is significant competition from businesses offering the same or similar services. Additionally, populated metropolitan areas may also be able to support an agency with a particular specialization. There are multiple examples of niche client populations in aging, and there are multiple opportunities for senior care businesses that specialize in a particular area of the market. An example of a niche client population could be cases where aging parents are themselves caregivers of mentally or developmentally disabled sons or daughters. Other niche populations could be aging clients with long-standing mental illness, non-elderly and elderly clients with traumatic brain injury, or end-of-life hospice home care.

Strategic Alliances with Complementary Businesses

Another take on the idea of "organization" that helps to build your home-based senior care business is the forming of an affiliation with other senior care providers. This concept is often referred to as a "strategic alliance." A strategic alliance is a partnering of businesses towards a goal of enhancing the performance of each of the participating businesses. The mutual effort can include group purchasing of commonly used supplies and equipment, or each business providing part of the overall service delivered to the end user. The basis for strategic alliances is to reduce cost and risk while increasing leverage in the marketplace. In their 1997 book *Teaming Up: The Small-Business Guide to Collaborating with Others to Boost Your Earnings and Expand Your Horizons*, Paul and Sarah Edwards mention activities such as networking, doing cross promotions, and joint venturing as examples of how businesses can form alliances.

One example of strategic alliance is a joint venture including an elder law attorney, a financial planner, and a geriatric care manager who arrange to do community forums on elder care planning from each of their professional purviews and business interests. The attorney might present on estate planning, while the financial planner presents on strategies for investing and accessing equity for financing elder care. The geriatric care manager finally presents an overview of elder care planning in terms of the physical problems encountered by frail elders and the resources and services that are typically obtained as part of a plan of care. Another example might involve a private-duty home care provider teaming up with an assisted-living facility where the home care agency provides extra care needed to allow the elderly residents of the facility to age in place.

Skills, Experience, Education, and Attitude

Owners of senior care businesses will need certain skills, knowledge, and experience in the combined areas of aging and health and in small business. While some aspiring senior care entrepreneurs will have ample knowledge and know-how to organize and run their businesses, many will have knowledge gaps in one or more of these areas.

An effective and grounded way to understand the type of senior care business that you are considering is to work in a business that provides the services that you seek to provide in your startup business. If no such position in a business with an identical (or at least similar) service line is available, then at minimum consider working in a business that serves seniors. Try to obtain a position that offers you the most opportunity to learn what you do not already know. Another way to gain experience in an organization that serves seniors is to take on a volunteer position or an unpaid or minimally paid internship. If you can afford not to earn a salary for a while (or to receive only a small stipend), a volunteer position or internship may allow for working in areas of an organization or on specialized projects that will provide you the specific knowledge or experience that you need.

Anne presents a fine example of working in a similar business in order to accrue needed knowledge and experience. Anne worked for years in direct practice nursing in hospitals, but after caring for several aging family members on her own time, she felt a yearning to start a home care agency focused on end-of-life care. To learn how to bill insurance for services rendered, Anne used her registered nursing credentials to land a position in the business office of an established home care agency. Despite her lack of relevant experience, the agency hired Anne for this position because she agreed to work half of her hours as an agency nurse. Fortunately, the agency for which Anne worked was somewhat out of the area where she lived and planned to start her own agency. After a few months she felt free to reveal her entrepreneurial plans to her boss, who offered to help her to understand the requisite business issues for running her own home care agency. Anne considered her ten months as an employee of that agency to be invaluable, and her experience there became the secret behind her quickly acquired success—well worth the cut in pay she took from her previous job as a hospital nurse.

Blending the Roles of Practitioner and Manager

Due to the fact that most senior care businesses deliver services to their clients, the issue of owner as practitioner and manager is particularly salient for senior care entrepreneurs. Owners of small businesses widely contend that it is necessary for the owner to have an up-to-date understanding of every facet of the business. A senior care business owner without knowledge of how well the organization is delivering service is at risk of losing customers, sometimes rapidly. In the world of services to seniors, success rests profoundly on the organization's (and sometimes the owner's) reputation. It is important that the owner fully understands what other professionals—such as accountants, attorneys, or independently contracted virtual assistants—are doing on behalf of the business.

A geriatric care manager colleague named Vicki recently spoke to me about competing private-duty home care agencies in her city. One agency is owned by a registered nurse who is in the office daily but at times seems only passively involved in important aspects of her agency activities, such as staffing and care planning. The nurse tends to delegate these matters to her paraprofessional staff. Vicki expressed that she finds working with this agency frustrating, because this sole owner with the bottom-line authority is often unavailable or unable to dialogue with her about serious issues facing their mutual clients.

Vicki explained further that the other private-duty home care agency is owned by a man named Kevin, a former investment banker who had no prior experience in aging or home care before buying his home care agency. Vicki said that Kevin hired a registered nurse to be the clinical manager of the agency, but also set out to learn as much as he could about his clients and their needs. Over the last few years, this agency, under Kevin's leadership, has developed innovative policies and practices that led to a competitive edge with referring professionals, such as hospital discharge planners and agency-based case managers. Vicki noted that a fellow elder care colleague in her city was surprised to learn that Kevin was the former banker.

She commented, "Based on Kevin's high level of care for his clients, I would have guessed that he was the nurse."

Educational Credentials and Certifications

As the senior care market expands, so do the number of senior care providers and the competition between them. Given this fact, impressive credentials and certifications will become increasingly important and may provide a competitive edge. Having said this, it is also important to be judicious as to which credentials or certifications to pursue. Professional certification and state licensing are areas that many health and human-services professionals can explore. There are credentials pertaining to the fields of social work, nursing, rehabilitation therapy, and mental health counseling. Additionally, there are some certifications available for home care agencies, and in many states licensure is required for home care agencies to operate, including those that are not Medicare certified. You will find a list with links to various certification organizations for some senior care–oriented services in the Resources section of this book.

Evaluating Professional or Business Credentials

- Is there any evidence that existing senior care businesses like the one I plan to start have this credential or designation? (Conduct a national search via the Internet.)

- Do professionals working in my senior care niche have the same credential? (Conduct a national search via the Internet.)

- Does the credentialing organization offer the same level of professional certification to applicants without related post-secondary education and experiences if they simply pay a fee, take a short course, and pass an exam given by the credentialing organization?

- Is the credential or designation recognized by elder care professionals that you know?

An example of the movement toward certification is the NAPGCM, which in 2006 instituted a requirement that all voting members of that organization be certified. The new rule requires that all members must hold at least one of four approved certifications, including Care Manager Certified (CMC), Certified Case Manager (CCM), Certified Advanced Social Worker in Case Management (C-ASWCM), and Certified Social Work Case Manager (C-SWCM). Membership with certification in this organization is vital for starting a professional geriatric care management practice.

I also urge caution when considering any kind of professional or business certification. With the rise in the senior care industry have come various "boiler room" credentialing operations preying on entrepreneurs. These unscrupulous operations may offer illegitimate certifications that are relatively easy to qualify for, often by simply paying a fee, joining an organization, or paying for scant elder care training. See the sidebar on page 11 for some tips on evaluating the legitimacy of certification programs.

Standards for Quality Service Are Vital

Perhaps the most important standard for a senior care business is the standard achieved, and then maintained, by the owner. Many startup senior care businesses involve a client or a client's agent paying out of pocket for your service. In some

System for Quality Checks

- Elicit feedback from clients and clients' agents via survey or independent phone or e-mail inquiry.

- Check in with clients (i.e., care recipients) through face-to-face visits and ask about their satisfaction.

- Get your clients' permission to have an objective third party sit down with them to get feedback regarding their level of satisfaction.

- Check in with other involved professionals, particularly the ones who referred the case.

- If your business includes staff providing service to clients, make surprise visits to clients while your employees are present.

senior care businesses, such as home care, there may be a very negligible difference in hourly rates among providers, so as a result the client will shop reputation over price. Building a reputation requires a passion for delivering quality services, and also a system for checking on the quality of the services that you are delivering.

Going Solo Versus Building an Organization

A major question for aspiring elder care entrepreneurs is whether to start a solo business or a business that will include the hiring of employees or subcontracted

Real Life Examples of Success

Adele is a forty-eight-year-old woman who had always dreamed of working for herself. Ten years ago, Adele helped a friend sort through the affairs of her mother, who had recently died. Adele found that she enjoyed and was particularly adept at organizing the various piles of outstanding bills, and was able to successfully advocate on her friend's behalf with insurance companies and medical providers regarding unpaid invoices. Based on the experience of helping her friend, Adele started her own organizing and bill-paying service for seniors. Adele charges $35 per hour and has a typical caseload of between seven and ten clients. Adele's home-based business is going so well that she occasionally has to place prospective clients on a waiting list.

Liam is a clinical social worker who had worked in a hospital setting for several years. At a conference, Liam met a man named Bob, who introduced him to the field of professional geriatric care management (GCM). Liam decided to embark on a GCM practice with two other social workers working out of a rented office. In a small amount of time it became clear to Liam that his idea of a group GCM practice was not working. Liam next decided to switch to a solo, home-based GCM practice. Through a year of very regular marketing activities including seminars, networking events, and marketing lunches, Liam started to obtain clients. He then spent some of his profits on an impressive Web site that promoted his business. After leaving his partners, Liam had identified what he considered to be a dream amount of money that he wanted to collect in monthly fees. He felt tremendous when he achieved that goal in less than eighteen months.

staff. This becomes an important question, as you may have strong feelings about working alone versus working with others. Most specializations in the field can work well as either a partnership or as a sole proprietorship with paid employees or independent contractors. It is common for geriatric care managers, psychotherapists, and senior-focused professional organizers to work in home-based solo businesses. On the other hand, a startup home care business may operate from the owner's home, at least in the initial stage, but would obviously involve hiring employees.

02

From Dreaming to Jumping In

In this next chapter and subsequent chapters I will move from the somewhat more general discussion in the first chapter to the specifics of starting a home-based senior care business. Perhaps the most basic question involves the location of your home-based office.

Locating and Furnishing Your Home Office

Where in your home will you locate your office? Situating your home office may take some discernment if you are lucky enough to have more than one option.

The work of a senior care business owner requires a significant amount of time on the phone. Given this, you should avoid locating your office where you might be distracted by household noise or activity, especially if these noises might be audible to the person with whom you are speaking over the phone. Clients and other professionals feel reassured when they have your undivided attention. I would also recommend that you install a separate business line in your home, and by all means do not use your home telephone as your business phone. While traditional land lines are becoming passé, a traditional business telephone line will give you a phone book listing. It will also allow less important calls to be answered by voice mail, while more important callers have access to your cell phone number.

For many senior care businesses, much of the work is "on the road," where you are visiting your elderly clients at home or in health facilities. Therefore, it is generally unnecessary to devote a lot of physical space and funds to office furnishings. A desk, computer (consider a laptop that can travel with you), telephone, and two- or three-drawer file cabinet are the office essentials that you will need. Even if you feel comfortable having client-oriented meetings in your home office, chances are that it will be more convenient and appropriate to conduct meetings in either a borrowed office or, more likely, a public location like a restaurant or coffee shop. Many senior care business owners will attest that they live by a reliable car and a cell phone—preferably a smart phone with access to the Internet and e-mail.

Identifying Your Target Client

As you begin to think about where and how to situate your home office, you should concurrently be thinking about your target client for your senior care business. Think about the discussions that you have had with other senior professionals and members of the general public. Review the notes that you took either during or after these discussions. Even without having yet served a client, become clear and articulate about what you do and for whom you do it. Practice your "elevator speech" (that is, how you would explain your business to a stranger in an elevator). Knowing this will give you the basis for developing your plan for marketing your startup business.

Budgeting

In this initial startup phase of your business, it is important to begin the process of budgeting. During the startup phase, expenses will generally be different than they will be once you are up and running. For example, fees for acquiring new supplies and equipment and printing are higher at startup, as opposed to the cost of fuel for your car and telephone charges, which are higher once you are serving clients. A distinct advantage to starting a home-based senior care business is that your startup costs need not be high, and you may already have or can easily obtain the equipment that you need for your business, such as basic office furniture. If possible, spend as little as you can on the items that are not immediately necessary. A good way to start is by looking at used office furniture and supplies online or at used office-furniture stores.

Presenting a Professional Appearance

A reliable and presentable automobile is probably a necessity, particularly if you will be transporting clients. Consider a lease as a way of getting more car for the money that you will pay out on a monthly basis. Speak to your accountant regarding strategies for writing off at least part of what you spend on car payments. Remember that you may need to alert your auto insurance agent that you will be using your

- A presentable and reliable automobile

- Neat and professional-looking clothing that is not ostentatious

- Office space in your home with a desk and file cabinet

- Fax machine and computer

- Office telephone line

- Cell phone, preferably a smart phone with e-mail and Internet access

- Printed business cards and brochures

- At least a basic Web site

automobile for business purposes and transporting clients in your car so that the proper rider can be added to your policy. These riders typically do not add much to the overall premium, are a write-off for business taxes, and are well worth it in terms of relieving you from liability in the event of an accident. While your car should appear neat and reliable, I would avoid purchasing or leasing an automobile that might be considered "too fancy" for your senior care business purposes.

I would suggest the same caution with regards to clothing. Dress neatly and professionally around clients. Male senior care professionals might consider always wearing a necktie when around clients. Having said this, excessive jewelry or fur coats, for example, may be inappropriate for your clientele. Remember, many of your elderly clients may be quite mindful of their experience of having lived through the Great Depression and may frown on a professional who is charging them for services yet has a too-opulent presentation.

Marketing Materials

The time and expense involved in printing business cards and brochures are necessary in the initial phase. You really cannot begin to market your business to members of the professional community or general public without these essential print materials. If you have a Web site, even if it's basic, put the address on your card and brochure. Consider printing a bookmark brochure, which will be far less costly and can direct potential clients or client agents to your Web site, where important information about you and your business is published. Every community has printing businesses that can assist you with this process. You may also want to speak to other entrepreneurs with small businesses about which printers they have been satisfied with. Given the importance of these startup items, you may want to stay away from lower-cost Web-based printing companies and instead opt for a local vendor, where you will have nearby access to the process and will be able to view physical proofs before they go into final printing.

A Web site is an expense that should be a priority at the startup phase. A Web site done right will enhance your image and may assure potential referral sources and clients that your business is established and is not "fly by night." If the cost of hiring a Web site designer and paying an additional technician to do optimization is too high at this startup phase, then consider going with a basic template site sometimes referred to as "brochure-ware." The important thing is that at the point of startup you have a Web presence declaring who you are and what you do.

Telephone Expenses

For many senior care entrepreneurs, telephone charges are an unavoidably high expense. While much can be done via e-mail, particularly with the long-distance relatives of clients working in office settings, much communication is still done over the phone. One reason for this is that sometimes the complexity of client issues and high level of collaboration needed between elder care professionals can best be handled via the telephone, or sometimes by conference call.

A business line in your home office is a necessity. I would recommend that you have telephone service with options for voice mail and for call-forwarding. The ability for your office phone calls to be forwarded to your cell phone means that you will not miss potentially urgent callers to your office phone. I would further suggest that you either have a separate cell phone for your business or set up the outgoing cell phone voice-mail message in a professional manner, even if you will also be taking personal calls on this phone. Always answer your phones with the name of your business and your name. While unlimited plans may have high monthly costs, you will likely find that once you are serving clients you will begin to see quite high fees for toll calls on your land line and will run through your contracted minutes quickly. Prepaying for a pricey unlimited plan for each phone may end up being more cost effective. (See Sample Monthly Business Expense Worksheet sidebar.)

Expense	Estimated Monthly Cost	x 12
Rent		
Utilities		
Telephone		
Bank fees		
Supplies		
Stationery and business cards		
Insurance		
Networking club and professional society dues		
Education (e.g., seminars, books, professional journals)		
Business car (e.g., payments, gas, repairs, insurance)		
Marketing		
Postage		
Entertainment		
Repair, cleaning, maintenance, and laundry		
Travel		
Business loan payments		
Licenses and permits		
Salary/draw		
Staff salaries/payroll expenses		
Taxes		
Professional fees		
Decorations		
Furniture and fixtures		
Equipment		
Inventory		
Other		
Total monthly		
Total yearly		

Budgeting Your Time

At the point that you are actively networking and marketing your business, you should also determine how many hours you can work in a week, and thus how much work you can take on. Most senior care professionals will attest to the fact that there is more time involved with opening a new client case, and also with handling periods of client crisis. If you bill for your time in increments, which is how many geriatric care managers (GCMs) and other elder care professionals bill, then you can expect that the real time that you work is an additional 25 to 50 percent of non-billable time over and above the billable time that you spend working on behalf of your client. So if you are still caring for young children at home or working another part-time or full-time job, you'll need to carefully monitor the time involved in serving one client before taking on more clients.

Given that elderly clients are sometimes not easily able to travel, it is often the case that the elder care professional needs to travel to his or her client. You need to assess your comfort and tolerance for driving or taking public transportation more than you ever have. If you are operating your home-based senior care business in a large metropolitan area, you might find that travel time involves taking public transportation or sitting in traffic. If you are operating in a rural or semirural area, you may find that you are putting a lot of miles on your car. For example, some GCMs practicing in rural areas are known to drive more than 25,000 miles per year just for work activities.

If you are undaunted by the prospect of business travel, you may also want to assess your tolerance for working in your office. Will your home-based office provide enough of a distraction-free environment that you will actually feel inclined to work in it? This is a crucial point for senior care professionals, because some very important matters often need to be tended to in an office setting, such as phone calls, progress notes, and other record keeping and client-oriented task planning. A senior care professional who is never in his or her office may be failing to identify and perform important proactive tasks on behalf of clients. Office work during off hours and weekends is a good way to catch up without the distraction of the telephone or e-mail, but it is important that your home office is usable during business hours as well.

Choosing a Specialization

Whether to specialize or be a generalist is an important decision to consider, both in the startup phase and also at a later date when you have learned more about serving seniors. There are all kinds of ways to specialize your senior care business, and successful specialties will require that there is market for that service and that you have the "know how" and desire to deliver that service. You may need to decide on a specialty area at startup, when there is already competition in the way of similar businesses offering similar services.

Before you consider specializing in any senior care specialty area, you should be sure that you will have the technical and personal facility for doing so. For instance, a startup elder home care entrepreneur might not want to specialize in end-of-life care if she finds herself becoming emotionally overwhelmed around clients who are in the process of dying.

See Appendix A for a description of some business titles found in the field of senior care along with relevant professional organizations and Web sites.

Staff

Another consideration for the startup phase is whether you will need staff, and how much. In most cases, the less staff the better, given the costs involved in hiring and maintaining employees. It is also important to realize that it is increasingly commonplace for businesses to outsource services that used to be handled by paid employees. This is particularly true for small businesses. Services such as bookkeeping, billing, and secretarial work can be done by independent contractors who work for other businesses as well. Sometimes it works well to hire an independent contractor who is also a home-based entrepreneur, and who possibly works in a geographic location with lower customary rates. These assistants are often identified as "virtual assistants" as they have only virtual contact with their customers.

In addition to contracted administrative or technical assistance, senior care entrepreneurs sometimes need higher-level clinical-oriented personnel who are independent contractors. Physical therapists, registered nurses, and clinical social workers are all clinicians who in most states can be licensed and insured to practice autonomously and can thus be contracted by the senior entrepreneur to serve a particular part-time role in the business.

It would be wise to locate administrative, technical, and clinical supports that you anticipate you will need once you begin to take on clients in your business. Interview possible administrative or technical assistants in person or virtually, and interview any fee-for-service clinicians, such as nurses or physical therapists, in person. To the extent possible, build your business as you anticipate your future needs. Then market like crazy in order to make the clients come!

03

Setting Up Your Office

Office Furniture

Set up your office thoughtfully; this should be a satisfying experience that is an expression of how you feel about your home-based senior care business. When choosing office furniture, avoid the latest and greatest. Senior care professionals are less likely than other businesspeople to be meeting with clients in their home offices, so there is no need to impress clients or client agents with fancy furniture.

Comfort is important, however; avoid uncomfortable or ill-fitting furnishings that will impede your desire to work in your office. Choose an office chair that can be set at the correct height for you for when you are writing or typing at your desk. Your desk should be large enough for you to lay out a client's file alongside other essentials such as a full-size notepad, phone, and clock. Elder care professionals who bill for their time want to avoid being slowed down by the wrong furniture. For example, poor office ergonomics can cause you to expend more time—and thus more of the client's money—by slowly writing e-mails and other documents.

Purchasing used office furniture can be an optimal way to obtain higher-quality items, such as desks, chairs, and filing cabinets, at a lower cost. Economic downturns are sometimes the best times for finding office furniture bargains.

Communication and Computers

Other office necessities include a phone, a reasonably up-to-date computer, and a fax machine. For elder care professionals who will be billing for their time, it is wise to purchase a phone that displays the elapsed time of a telephone call. This will help you keep track of your billable time.

A fax machine may sound out of date, but it is a necessary office item. While most documents are now sent back and forth via e-mail, many official documents containing signatures, such as medical release forms and court documents, cannot easily be e-mailed. Additionally, many organizations will not permit documents to be e-mailed due to the concern that they can be altered. Any senior care professional will attest to the fact that attorney and physician offices continue to rely heavily on fax machines. It is best to have a dedicated phone line for your fax machine, although this need not be a more expensive business line. This dedicated line can be an additional home phone line.

Acquiring an up-to-date computer for your business is essential. This is because you want to have a computer that will "grow with you" as you add applications such as management and communication software. Remember that senior care professionals often interface regularly with the relatives of clients who may be working at state-of-the-art offices during business hours, and it is important to know that out-of-date technology will not compromise your ability to communicate with them.

If you are going to purchase a new computer, consider whether a laptop is the best solution. The advantage of a laptop is, of course, the portability. A disadvantage is that laptop or notebook computers have historically been known to perform less reliably, although increasingly this is less true. The other disadvantage to using a laptop computer for a senior care business is the possibility of it being lost or stolen with highly confidential client information on it.

A factor to consider is whether the computer has an application that can synch with your smart phone or Blackberry, allowing you to send and receive e-mail and make notes while on the go. Finally, if it is at all affordable, purchase a new computer designed for business, as these types of computers often come with business-oriented software already loaded. Otherwise, you may have to purchase this pricy software separately, which is often necessary when adapting a computer meant for "home users."

Software

Word Processing

Acquiring the right computer software is a necessary part of owning and operating a startup business. First, word processing software is used to create documents. It is perhaps the most frequently used software program. Microsoft Word is a ubiquitous word processing program, and I would suggest purchasing it for that reason.

Microsoft Word comes bundled with a larger software package called Microsoft Office, which includes other important programs for creating spreadsheets, as well as PowerPoint, which creates slides used in presentations.

Another recommended software program is Adobe Acrobat. This program converts word processing documents into Portable Document Format, or PDF. PDFs are useful because nearly every computer already has the software required to read PDFs. This resolves the problem of a receiver not being able to open a document written on a word processing program that his or her computer does not recognize. Sending documents in PDF format is more official and secure, particularly when they are encrypted for security, or digitally signed for authentication.

In addition to Adobe, CutePDF (www.cutepdf.com) has a free application that creates PDF documents from any word processing application. This application claims to enable the creation of a PDF document from any printable document, such as Microsoft Word documents, spreadsheets, or Web pages.

E-mail

E-mail is an essential part of communication in business today, and the senior care industry is no exception. E-mail and increasingly text messaging are particularly effective for breaking the chain of phone tag that so often occurs when busy professionals are also spending office time on the phone. Microsoft Outlook is an e-mail program that offers other useful features including a calendar. Another advantage of Microsoft Outlook is that you can use it in conjunction with certain smart phones, such as a Blackberry. By connecting it to the computer with a cable, you can synchronize all of the content on a Blackberry device, including contact information, notes, and calendar entries, with Microsoft Outlook and vice versa.

Business Management Software

Business management software exists for all kinds of businesses and all kinds of applications. Most small home-based businesses are able to run their offices based on some of the most popular software designed for management, such as Quicken.

Quickbooks is a widely used accounting system today. It claims to offer a full accounting package and can run your business from end to end. Quickbooks can be used to track customers, invoices, expenses, accounts receivable, and payables. Quickbooks is also able to track your employees' payroll and taxes, produce financial statements, and create budgets, cash flow estimates, and profit-and-loss statements. Quickbooks can be purchased as a stand-alone application, or you can subscribe to Quickbooks online as a monthly service. This can be useful if you work from different locations, and want to be able to access your accounting data from any computer. It is much simpler to use the Quickbooks system if the setup is properly completed, so you should hire an accountant or professional to set it up. Your accountant can easily work with Quickbooks data and manipulate it at the end of the year for tax purposes. You can learn more about Quickbooks by logging on to www.intuit.com.

Other software options for managing your senior care business include online billing and management tools. Cashboard (www.getcashboard.com) offers an online subscription service for time-based billing. Cashboard can be used as a stand-alone application to invoice customers and collect payments, or it can be combined with its sister project management software Basecamp (www.basecamphq.com). Basecamp and Cashboard together offer the ability to track cases as projects, keep all of your notes in one place on a particular client or case, and retain contact information and "to do" items in one spot. Invoices in Cashboard can be electronic or printed to be sent via regular mail. The invoices and the look of the application can be customized to your business. These applications can be synched with a Blackberry and have their own applications for iPhones. The service pricing is flexible based on how large your clientele is and can be changed at any time to accommodate growth or downsizing.

There are also some widely used management software programs designed for certain senior care businesses. Care Manager Pro and Jewel Code are both proprietary software programs designed for geriatric care managers (GCMs). Each program continues to grow in subscribers, along with the number of GCMs entering the field and joining the National Association of Professional Geriatric Care Managers. John, a GCM, recently spoke to me about his experience with Care Manager Pro. He uses this program to record the activities that he performs on behalf of clients, and then convert that information into professional-looking invoices that he sends to his clients each month. Additionally, he relies on Care Manager Pro to generate reports on different aspects of his business, including year-to-date earnings. John explained to me that Care Manager Pro also has numerous forms available that were created to assist a GCM in both business and clinical arenas. Given the overall utility of that one brand of care management software, it seems prudent that any senior care specialist thoroughly survey available software that might be specifically tailored for your particular type of senior business.

Printers, Copiers, and Shredders

A printer is an absolute necessity for your home office. With regards to the purchase of a printer, you tend to get what you pay for. Additionally, while "all-in-one" style printer, fax, and plain page copiers are very affordable, you will gradually become outraged by the amount of money that you are spending on replacement printer cartridges. An alternative to a low-cost printer is a laser jet printer. Laser jet printers perform better. Additionally, while the up-front cost of purchasing a laser printer will be higher, over time you will likely save money given the many more copies you will get from the toner cartridge of a laser jet printer. For example, prior to the purchase of my laser jet printer, I would typically run through a black ink cartridge for my all-in-one printer in matter of four to six weeks at a cost of about $25 per ink cartridge. By contrast, I replaced the black toner cartridge in my laser jet after over one year of use for approximately $80. If you want to save money by purchasing a lower-cost office machine, consider a very basic home office glass-top photocopier, which you might find for less than $200.

Another essential office machine for the senior care entrepreneur is a paper shredder. I would highly recommend purchasing as high-end a shredder as you can afford, as small business owners often attest to the sudden failure of paper shredders due to overuse. The increase of stories in the news regarding identity theft underscores the importance of always shredding and never simply discarding papers with identifying information about your clients or yourself.

Paper Supplies for Your Home-Based Office

- File holders
- 8½ x 11 paper files (consider using varying colors for different file types)
- Paper for your copier and printer
- Nicer bond paper with your letterhead for more formal correspondence
- Desktop supplies such as scissors, tape, paperclips, a return address stamp, stationery with your letterhead, and matching blank bond paper

Forms

Forms are part of any business and are especially important in a senior care service business. It is vital that legitimate parties sign forms authorizing services and the receipt and dissemination of information prior to service commencing. There are various ways to put together a packet of forms that are to be reviewed and signed by the client or the client's agent. One way is to purchase forms. Numerous Web sites sell general business forms online, which you can tailor for your business.

You will also need forms that are specific to the service area of your senior care business. There are ways to get those forms as well, which can include offering to purchase a set from a competitor or someone doing the same service as you out of your area. In some cases a professional organization might have forms that you can purchase. For example, NAPGCM offers a forms book containing ninety forms in areas such as assessment, intake, money management, and mental status for $125. This forms book is also available in an electronic format so you can tailor each form for your senior care business. The GCM forms book could be applicable to other senior care businesses in addition to GCM. Finally, as your senior care business grows and develops, you may find that the forms with the most utility are the forms that you create yourself.

04

The Business Plan: Your Plan of Action

It is typically standard practice for startup businesses to create a business plan. There are several reasons to formulate a business plan. First, a business plan is a way for the aspiring entrepreneur to put his or her grand vision down on paper. It can be a portable reference that describes the planned complete "build out" of the business, as well as planned prior phases for the business. A business plan should be alive and come from the heart.

A business plan must also be changeable, as you cannot predict the future. There are trends that often affect senior care businesses, such as a dwindling number of elders in a specific geographic area who can afford to pay privately for services.

Sometimes either direct or indirect competition might necessitate a change in a business plan. For example, Harry, a carpenter, was setting up a business offering home modifications for disabled people who wanted to remain at home, including the installation of grab bars, widening doorways, and construction of ramps to accommodate residents in wheelchairs. Harry recently learned that another carpenter named Dan had just launched a very similar home modification business and would be a direct competitor. Additionally, a large retirement community offering independent and assisted living including subsidized units as well as skilled nursing care was being constructed in Harry and Dan's city. This project was an indirect competitor for both businesses, as it offered an alternative for disabled elders who might be reluctant to lay out thousands of dollars on home modifications in order to remain in their own homes when this cost would likely not be recoverable when the home was sold. Clearly Harry would want to be sure that his business plan included the kinds of services and modifications that would apply to both home and community residences in order for him to stay competitive.

Any business plan written by the aspiring entrepreneur should be heartfelt, but also based on educated assumptions about the market that can be documented. For example, Judy, a nurse, considered starting a geriatric care management practice in her local area, which had a major state university but was mostly rural. She had been researching the care management field, including trends suggesting that GCM was a service needed throughout the nation. Judy was, however, getting mixed reviews when she proposed her care management practice idea to business leaders in her community as well other health care professionals. Several professionals expressed concern to Judy that the community might not be ready for a professional service that involved a relatively high out-of-pocket cost.

Given this feedback, Judy devised what she contended would be predictive market research. She first analyzed certain key demographic data about her community, such as household income and percentage of adults in the community who were older than seventy-five years of age. Judy next compared the statistics regarding her community to communities in other parts of the United States and identified a few that were very close demographic matches to her own community. Using the "Find a Care Manager" application on www.caremanager.org, the Web site for the National Association of Professional Geriatric Care Managers, Judy contacted several GCMs in those similar areas. Judy offered to pay some of the GCMs for telephone consultations. In these consultations Judy asked market research questions pertaining to the GCMs' experience of getting started and conducting initial marketing, as well as the rate that business grew over time. Judy took copious notes during these consultations, and then summarized this information and presented it as market analysis and market projections in her business plan.

A business plan essentially "counts down" the time pertaining to the short- and long-term goals of your business through a planning process. Once the business plan is completed, it should not be stowed away but instead regularly reviewed and changed as often as needed. Your business plan should always be your call to action for your employees, or a way to communicate your goals to the outside world. It should cover a specific time frame—often the first six to twelve months. Your business plan can be a great tool for meetings with bankers when you are attempting to secure a business loan or a business credit line. This is because a business plan, done right, will succinctly provide a general description of the business as well as its goals and objectives. It will explain how clients will be served fully, and how this competitive edge will result in continuing higher levels of new business and profitability. In addition to explaining to potential financiers a plan for growth and development, the business plan can also include some specifics regarding the marketing plan and financial plan.

A good way to get started on your business plan is to ask yourself about the kind of results that you would like the business plan to have. In order to illustrate this process of developing a business plan, I will introduce the example of an aspiring senior care entrepreneur named Nicole. Nicole is a thirty-four-year-old mother of two very young children. Nicole and her husband both work full-time at highly demanding jobs in New York City's financial district. Each of them earns similarly high salaries and works about fifty hours per week, commuting an additional ten to fifteen hours to work by train.

In the past year, Nicole lost her mother to Parkinson's disease. The prior twelve months leading up to the death of Nicole's mother were an arduous time for Nicole and her siblings. Her mother, who was receiving around-the-clock care at home, began to dramatically lose weight and become medically unstable, including experiencing difficulties with swallowing. Over time, Nicole and her siblings made the difficult decision to move their mother into a skilled nursing facility, where she died after a few months. Nicole explained to me that on some level she knew that her mother was dying, yet she and her siblings held out hope, which complicated their process of planning.

Nicole also fell into the role of handling many of her mother's business affairs, which included interfacing with her mother's attorney and accountant as well as the staff of the local hospital and nursing facility, such as doctors, nurses, and social workers. While Nicole found some aspects of her mother's end-of-life care to be quite positive, she also became very frustrated along the way. One of the more profound challenges Nicole experienced in terms of helping her mother was dealing with her mother's health insurance and prescription medication coverage, as well as charges from hospitals and health facilities and from physicians and labs. Nicole's siblings relied on her to resolve these problems on behalf of their mother, and were quite impressed with her ability to organize this rather complex information and to understand it within the context of insurance benefits.

One Sunday afternoon some months after her mother died, Nicole took some time to reflect on how much she had learned from the experience of being an advocate for her mother. She considered how much she had grown to dread her very demanding job, and how much she would like to be self-employed, working from home and being more available to her young children. And that Sunday afternoon, Nicole began to envision herself in her private home-based consulting business where she would provide medical insurance and billing advocacy services on behalf of elderly and disabled clients.

Nicole desired to create a business plan partly as a process that would help get her thoughts straight as to how she wanted her business to be. Her plan would also serve as a well-written document that she could shop around to various bankers as she sought financing or a credit line. Nicole knew that she wanted her business plan to be concise, to convey a compelling personal story (her own), and to predict that she could possibly change the lives of her soon-to-be clients. She also wanted her business plan to project growth and the possibility for enough expansion to include associates working for her. Nicole also knew that the process of business planning would take her through the steps of doing a necessary analysis of her potential market. Finally, she relished the thought of beginning to establish short- and long-term goals for her business. Nicole also mentioned on a personal note that she wanted to have something in writing that she could show her husband to give him some confidence that she had a good next step to take before she gave notice of wanting to resign from her highly paid position at the brokerage firm.

Executive Summary

The executive summary is an important first component of a business plan. It is meant to summarize the business idea, and it should be written for a reader who might be a banker, an investor, or someone else of prominence. Nicole began her executive summary by stating how overwhelming it has become to deal with medical billing and insurance companies on behalf of individuals who are chronically disabled and terminally ill. She also explained that family members and friends, and even other professionals who try to advocate on behalf of care recipients, find themselves spending significant amounts of time and experiencing stress as they are forced to learn about policies and procedures that are complicated and often nonsensical. Finally Nicole also expressed that many family members in the roles of medical insurance advocates would gladly turn to an expert for help.

Business Description

The next section of the business plan is generally called the business description; the business description describes the type and purpose of the business. It discusses the mission and goals of the business, as well as the potential value it will have for customers and a description of the services it offers. The business description should be informative and written in plain language with a tone that would inspire a reader. The purpose of the business description is to discuss in objective terms your senior service idea in a positive and compelling way.

Nicole thought about the ownership, organization, and management of her startup senior care business. She thought about the ages of clients in her local community that she knew she could serve well. Nicole was confident that the fee she was charging on an hourly basis would be affordable to enough people that she would be able to find an ample clientele to keep her as busy as she wanted to be in this business. She visualized working at home with a child caregiver in her home minding her children, but also having at least some visual access to them during the course of the day.

Nicole thought more about the rationale for her business. She knew she needed to justify to a potential investor that there would be a market for her services. She thought that one ready way to do this would be to get some idea of the number of families that were in her local community that were in situations similar to the one that she and her siblings had experienced not too long ago. With this question in mind, Nicole employed a simple, grounded strategy for market analysis. Nicole called four area skilled nursing facilities and asked the social worker in each of these facilities if she could take him or her out to lunch in order to introduce them to her business idea. Over the course of these four lunch meetings, Nicole discussed the situation that her family had recently gone through with her mother and then described what she hoped to do in her medical insurance advocate service. Nicole also very specifically asked the social workers to estimate the number of families that they thought had highly complex medical insurance issues that needed to be resolved, and to assess those families' interest and the ability to hire a consultant. On average, Nicole was told by the social workers that on a monthly basis three to six new families had some kind of a discussion with them about their difficulties dealing with insurance reimbursement, and that they felt these family members would be relieved to know that there was a professional in the community who could help them with that problem. Nicole thought that if one client from each facility was referred to her each month, before long she would be as busy as she hoped to be in her up-and-coming home-based senior care business.

An important facet to consider as you begin to assemble the information for your business plan is the purpose and the description of the services you will actually offer. In other words, what is it you want to do in this business? In Nicole's case, she did not have a precise answer to this beyond the very direct experience she had working on behalf of her mother and her family. She knew that she spent countless hours on the phone with insurance companies, seeing to it that charges that seemed as if they should be covered were indeed covered, or if not, that she understood the reasons why. Additionally, in the case of her mother's pharmacy coverage, she had worked with her mother's physicians to have them write letters on her mother's behalf to push for her mother to be able to use experimental and name-brand drugs.

Over the months that Nicole's mother was gravely ill, her role as an advocate continued. As she became increasingly daunted by errors that she noticed in bills, she felt inspired to make calls to medical providers and insurance companies when she had a free moment at work. When Nicole thought about the service she could provide to her clients, she thought about the fact that when she first started to help her mother she took a sort of inventory of her mother's insurance policies, read the benefits books very carefully, and understood the provisions for each aspect of these policies and called the insurance companies to see if there were any modifications. She then developed a system for organizing correspondence, such as explanations of benefits.

Nicole used her computer to organize and tabulate the amounts of the invoices that were paid to the medical providers and pharmacies by her mother's Medicare and supplemental HMO policy, as well as amounts paid by her mother's pharmacy coverage for pharmacy bills. Nicole felt she could offer something very similar to her clients. In an initial meeting, she would take a sort of inventory of the client's insurance policies. Additionally, Nicole thought it might be good for her to take the time to learn possible options for insurance coverage she could recommend for clients whom she determined to be underinsured. Nicole was sure that she could take copies of a client's existing outstanding bills and then develop an arrangement so that she could get copies of subsequent bills and relieve this complicated task from her disabled clients and their emotionally overwhelmed family members.

So, given that Nicole had the experience of providing medical billing and insurance advocacy on behalf of her mother and her family, a description of her startup business emerged rather easily. She developed the following description of services to her clients:

- To determine health insurance benefit provisions and limitations
- To carefully monitor or research reimbursements
- To engage in telephone- or computer-based interactions with health insurance representatives to resolve errors and delays with payments
- To offer a system for ongoing monitoring of health insurance matters for her clients

Ownership, Organization, and Management

In preparing the business plan, it is important to think about the ownership, organization, and management of your business. Nicole was clear that she wanted this to be her own business, and settled on a single-owner LLC (limited liability company) type of corporate structure (look for more about various ways to incorporate in the next chapter).

Operating Plan

The description of how you run your business is called the operating plan.

Nicole thought about the timing and when she wanted her business to officially start. She considered the kinds of resources that she anticipated needing in order to get started, including supplies, equipment, and financial capital. Nicole thought that she might need to hire an independent contractor to do certain administrative tasks, but for the first year anticipated that she would essentially be running her business herself.

The operating plan also describes the physical necessities of your business operation, such as where the office is located and the equipment that you will be using to run your business. Nicole knew that she would need certain key pieces of equipment for the office that she planned to set up in the finished basement of her home. Nicole already had a computer, but she thought that this might be the occasion to purchase an updated computer with a suite of business-oriented software already loaded on it. She wanted to shop around to see if there were any software applications that could help her in her work as a medical billing advocate.

Nicole also needed a filing cabinet, a reliable fax machine, a high-quality printer, and a good shredder. Based on the experience she had with her mother, she knew that she would be dealing with a lot of paper, as she would be acquiring paper copies of medical bills, statements, and explanations of benefits for each of her clients. Nicole also realized that she needed a piece of equipment that is not so widely used—a portable scanner. With a portable scanner Nicole would not need to take away her clients' paperwork temporarily in order to make copies and then return them, risking the possibility of papers being lost.

Goals

It is important to be clear about your goals throughout the process of creating a business plan. At the startup phase, you will likely be focusing on marketing goals. Think about the description of your market, the image that you hope to create for your startup business, and the position you want it to have within the market. In doing some research, Nicole could not find any other professional in her area offering a service similar to what she had planned. She did, however, find a national Web site offering training and an association for people doing medical advocacy.

Successful entrepreneurs will tell you that you should avoid dreaming too small. If you have an idea for an income that you would like to make and a total revenue that you would like your startup business to achieve in the first year, put that number down on a piece of paper. Look at it often and don't be afraid to go for it. You should also know your business well enough to be able to understand the kind of metric it would take to reach that number—thus, the number of clients served, the number of billable hours provided, and so on. You'll have to expend a lot of your initial effort on startup-oriented activities, such as setting up an office, acquiring supplies and equipment, putting together print and electronic materials, and acquiring clients. Once you begin to get business, of course, you will always have to continue to do regular marketing in order to stay vibrant and ahead of the competition.

Nicole decided that she could work close to full-time in her medical billing and insurance advocacy business, even in the startup phase when she wasn't going to be drawing much of an income. She didn't want to let up on the momentum that she had built up from years of working in New York City full-time. She made an arrangement with her child-care providers to cut back on child care, while still allowing herself twenty-five to thirty hours per week to devote to her business. Nicole decided that she wanted her business plan to include the attainment of one new ongoing client for each month in the coming year. By the end of a year's time she would have at least twelve active clients. From her experience with her mother, Nicole figured that on average she would be able to perform one to two billable hours on each client per week. Therefore, in her twelfth month she would be serving twelve clients for an average of eighteen billable hours per week. She knew that she could use the balance of her time to market and further develop her business.

Financial Assumptions

Nicole's exercise in financial assumptions is an important matter to think through, as making financial assumptions in a startup business relying on private fees is not a very easy task. Many business owners worry about whether their business can be profitable enough fast enough to offset regular payments that need to be made for initial capital expenses, such as real estate and capital equipment. Additionally, many service-based startup businesses take on the challenge of producing a profit fast enough to make up for lost income from the owner's previous job. One way to control that risk is to use your business plan to get a credit line, and then to pay yourself from that credit line. Keep in mind, however, that all borrowed funds will generate income tax liability. Additionally, this borrowed money will accrue interest, which you will have to pay back along with principle. Thus, it is a bit risky to rely on your credit line as your source of income even for just a short time. Perhaps a reasonable financial assumption to make in your startup senior care business is that you hope to recoup initial costs spent on startup-related expenses and be profitable enough to pay yourself a very minimal salary once you've been up and running for six months.

Estimate of Startup Costs

The presentation of an estimate of startup costs should be a feature of a business plan. Many experts identify certain categories of startup costs. A first category involves the cost of production. In a small service-oriented business this cost might be low. Nicole did not consider that there was an actual cost of producing her service, as she personally possessed the skills necessary for this. By contrast, Harry, the carpenter with a home modifications business, anticipated that he would have significant material costs, particularly for building materials.

Startup businesses will inevitably incur costs for professional fees. These fees were fortunately low for Nicole, as she only needed the services of her accountant to set up the structure for her business (an LLC). Other startup senior care businesses might also require the services of an attorney who specializes in business matters. Technology costs are part of the startup phase of any business. For senior care entrepreneurs, technology-related startup costs can include computer hardware and software, a printer, scanner, fax machine, office phones, and a cell phone or personal data assistant (PDA) such as a Blackberry. Web site development and maintenance, Web site optimization, high-speed Internet access, servers, and security measures may also be necessary startup expenses.

Administrative costs such as professional and business liability insurance, office supplies, postage, and licenses and/or permits are typical startup costs as well; however, some administrative costs such as parking, rent, and utilities are typically not an issue for a home-based entrepreneur. There are some one-time or infrequent startup costs associated with setting up a home-based office, such as a desk, chair, filing cabinets, or any other item you will be using on a daily basis for operating your business. Marketing costs—particularly the cost of printing stationery and other marketing materials such as brochures and business cards, as well as possibly some initial advertising and public relations campaigns—need to be factored in as requisite startup costs. Given the relationship between professional networking and marketing, the cost of memberships for trade associations or the local chamber of commerce is an important startup expense, as are fees for conferences and related travel expenses. Many senior care entrepreneurs may also want to budget funds for meals or entertainment for potential referral sources in the startup phase. Finally, senior care entrepreneurs who will be taking on employees must consider the costs associated with wages and benefits as well as payroll taxes, workers' compensation, and unemployment insurance.

While Nicole was not intending to hire employees, she knew that many of the above startup costs were going to apply to her medical billing and insurance advocacy business, including costs associated with creating a Web site; obtaining suitable office machines such as a computer, printer, and fax machine; purchasing a PDA; and finally designing and producing print materials for marketing, such as brochures and business cards.

Profit and Loss and Break-Even Point

Considering profit and loss potential and a break-even point is an important feature of a business plan for a startup business. Determining the break-even point as accurately as possible will inform the owner as to how profitable—or not—his or her startup business is.

The determination of the break-even point looks at certain factors. The first is the revenue that a business receives for a unit of service. Most, but not all, senior care businesses provide services and bill in a unit of time for services rendered, such as hours or parts of hours. So in the case of a senior care business billing for time, the unit price received is the amount that is charged for a unit of service. When considering the price that your business will charge for time, consider if the rate will vary depending on the time of the day or the day of the week. For instance, many home care agencies charge higher hourly rates for evening, overnight, weekend, and holiday shifts. Nicole established a $90-per-hour fee that would be billed to her clients in ten-minute units. Therefore, a unit price received for her medical insurance advocacy business is $15 ($90 per hour divided by six ten-minute units per hour equals $15).

The second factor for determining a break-even point is the average per unit cost. For most senior care businesses, this is the cost of providing a unit of time of service to a client. Average per-unit cost is often an overall variable figure for startup service-based businesses, due to the fact that the cost of doing business tends to reduce with the number of clients served and thus units of service delivered. In considering her per-unit cost, Nicole figured that the average cost for her to provide service to her clients would be reduced as the number of clients she served—and thus the number of hours of service she provided—increased along with the revenue her business would thus generate. In order to calculate the average per-unit cost, Nicole added up what she expected to pay for as a one-time expense in the startup phase. These costs included a computer, office machines, office furniture, and professional fees associated with incorporation. While she planned to use her credit line for these purchases, it was her goal to pay for these items within twelve months. Given this goal, she calculated the total cost of these one-time purchases and then divided this figure by twelve months. Nicole carefully estimated that the total cost for one-time startup expenses would be $12,000. She then divided this figure by twelve months and determined that her monthly obligation for these one-time startup costs for the first year would be $1,000.

Nicole then carefully estimated the ongoing costs that she would be incurring in her business. This included automobile expenses, communications charges (e.g., Internet connection and PDA service), and insurance premiums. Nicole established that these ongoing costs were likely going to reach $600 per month, but she also acknowledged that some of these costs would increase with usage, so they would increase as her business grew.

With a total predicted $1,600 per-month overhead cost, Nicole calculated that she would need to provide about 17.8 hours of service, or forty-seven ten-minute units of service, in order to break even for each month. If Nicole's average productivity through her first year averaged only forty-seven units of service per month, then using a basic forecast table, the percentage estimate for her business would determine a 0 percent margin of profit. As explained earlier, Nicole had predicted that within a year's time she would be doing on average eighteen billable hours per week in her business. Given this goal, Nicole thought it realistic to predict that she would be billing about half that many hours per week on average over the course of the initial twelve-month period, thus, nine hours per week or fifty-four units per week. Nicole then multiplied 54 units per week by 4.3 weeks per month (the actual average number of weeks in a month) and established a predicted average delivery of 232 units of service per month. Given Nicole's established monthly break-even point of 47 units of service per month and her predicted average delivery of 232 units of service per month, she calculated that her profit margin would be approximately 80 percent, or 0.8.

While Nicole's prediction may seem overly optimistic for a startup senior care business, Nicole's estimation essentially conforms with the profitability of many other successful solo entities in which the owner is also the primary provider of direct services. It is, however, very important to note that while the profit margins can be high for small home-based businesses with relatively low overhead, the overall revenue is limited to the amount of business the solo owner can attract and his or her ability to produce. This business model is thus limited when contrasted with larger businesses with employees or associates who are also providing direct service along with or instead of the owner. While costs significantly increase for the startup business with staff, so does the overall potential for productivity and profit. For example, some home care agencies report an overhead of nearly 85 percent, yet they also report a robust ability to attract clients, and their business growth is only limited by a lack of available candidates for employment. So while a startup home care agency may have a profit margin of only 15 percent, it may have the potential to generate far more profit than Nicole's one-woman home-based business.

Given that you purchased this book, you are likely planning to start your business on a small scale, and possibly have it be home-based. You should remember that many home-based businesses, even though small, can be quite profitable, and many home-based business owners make a choice to remain located at home even after considerable success because they want the convenience and savings that such arrangements provide.

Types of Company Ownership

Home-based businesses do, however, need a measure of formality involving incorporation in order to appear established, to engage in proper financial reporting and payment of taxes and fees, and most important, to minimize financial and legal risk. Startup businesses can choose to form either a limited liability company (LLC) or a corporation, such as an S corporation or a C corporation.

Sole Proprietorship or Partnership

Before giving a more detailed description of the above ways to structure a business entity, it is important to discuss other business arrangements, some of which were pretty common for small businesses operating in the United States at one time. First, a sole proprietorship owned by one person is a way to establish a one-owner business. In a sole proprietorship the owner may operate his or business solo, or may have employees. It is important to note, however, that the owner in a sole proprietorship has complete, unlimited personal liability for any debt incurred by the business. Similar to a proprietorship, a partnership involves an entity in which two or more people operate a business with the common goal of making profit. As is the case in a proprietorship, each of the partners assumes unlimited personal liability for any debt incurred by the partnership.

The unlimited personal liability involved with sole proprietorships and general partnerships can be mitigated with the formation of a limited liability company (LLC) or limited liability partnership (LLP). I will discuss LLCs and LLPs later in this chapter.

Benefits of Incorporation

Despite its small size, a home-based business can benefit from forming an LLC or corporation. Perhaps the most important benefit involves the ability of the **entrepreneur to protect his or her personal assets as owners of a corporation** or LLC, as he or she may separate corporate assets from personal assets, which remain protected. Another advantage from the standpoint of public relations and marketing is the **legitimacy gained by having the term "Inc." or "LLC" after the name of your business.** This may lead to a competitive advantage with organizations offering similar services but lacking this legitimacy. Furthermore, in **many states another entity may not use the name of an already incorporated business, which also adds to legitimacy.**

When a business is incorporated, the owner has a certain amount of flexibility with regard to paying taxes, including avoiding paying double taxes (in the case of S corporations and LLCs).** Incorporated businesses such as corporations and LLCs can also deduct business expenditures before they allocate profit to the owner. Finally, **by incorporating, your business can continue to exist even if the ownership of your businesses changes.** By contrast, a sole proprietorship or partnership simply ends in the event of the death or departure of a partner or owner.

Corporations

A corporation is any for-profit business that is separate from the personal financial existence of its sole owner or its partners. A board of directors controls an incorporated business, except in the case of cooperatives, or "co-ops." Co-ops are corporations owned by multiple shareholders. A cooperative is a for-profit entity with members directing its operations, instead of shareholders who share limited liability.

Corporations can be formed as either C corporations or subchapter S corporations. C corporations are formed at the state level and provide limited liability for the debts and obligations of the corporate owners. A C corporation can continue to exist after the original founders have left or died and can have an unlimited number of owners, and the owners need not be U.S. citizens or residents. A C corporation can be owned by another business rather than by individual owners, and can issue stock to attract investors. Owners of a C corporation can also split profit and loss in order to obtain a lower overall tax rate.

S corporations differ from C corporations in that they are limited to no more than one hundred owners or shareholders, the owners need to be U.S. citizens, and the corporation cannot be owned by another business. While owners of an S corporation cannot split profit and loss in order to obtain a lower overall tax rate, S corporations are more akin to partnerships in terms of taxation as income—deductions and tax credits flow through to the owners regardless of whether the owners were paid any amount of profit. The income of an S corporation is thus taxed at the owner's tax rate and not at a corporate level, and distributions to S corporation owners by the corporation are made tax-free, since these earnings were previously taxed. Additionally, some tax penalties, such as the alternative minimum tax, accumulated earnings tax, and personal holding company tax, do not apply to S corporations. The bottom line here is that owners of S corporations escape the double tax situation (i.e., taxes paid by the corporation and then taxes paid on the owner's personal income from income received by the corporation). It is, however, important to emphasize that an attorney or accountant should always be consulted regarding questions of incorporation, as in some cases there may be advantages related to limiting liability and paying taxes as a C corporation instead of an S corporation.

Limited Liability Companies

LLCs (or in some cases LLPs when partners are involved) are becoming the most popular type of incorporation for smaller businesses due to the tax advantages, flexibility, and optimal personal legal liability protection. LLCs are now the standard type of incorporation, as compared to S corps and C corps. Although the structure of LLCs may vary from one state to another, there are generally several common features of LLCs. These include the following:

- Owners have limited liability for business debts.
- LLCs are created at the state level, which usually protects the business name.
- LLCs can have an unlimited number of owners.
- Owners of an LLC need not reside in the U.S. nor be citizens.
- LLCs may be owned by another business.
- Owners can report profit and loss on their personal tax returns.

- LLCs can make special distributions under some guidelines (i.e., partners are not required to divide profit and loss according to percentage of ownership).
- Partners of an LLC are not required to have and record the proceedings of corporate meetings.

The cost to incorporate is not overly high, and certainly worth it from the standpoint of liability protection. Fees for incorporating and filing vary from state to state. Typical costs include filing fees, annual report fees, attorney fees for up-front costs associated with the formation of the corporation, and first-year franchise taxes (these range between $800 and $1,000, but are not required in all states for all corporate structures). Fees for annual reports vary from state to state but generally range from $50 to $600. Some states require all businesses to obtain a business license, which is typically not expensive. Finally, some states require a newly incorporated entity to remit a publication fee of a few hundred dollars.

Business Licenses

A business license grants legal authorization for a business to operate in a city, county, or state, or sometimes on a federal level. For example, a business that offers financial investment advice to seniors may have to obtain a federal business license. A business license grants the right of a senior care business to conduct the services described in the licensing application. There is typically a fee associated with obtaining a business license. It is important to note that some locales allow small home-based businesses such as senior care businesses to operate without a license. Entrepreneurs should research whether a license is needed for a particular business at the federal, state, or local level. With regards to a local requirement for licensing, it is also important for startup entrepreneurs with businesses that are home-based to check local zoning laws, as in some areas zoning restrictions may exist.

Another type of license is a professional license. These traditionally apply to lawyers, dentists, and doctors. Some senior care businesses may be owned by professionals who are required to have a license. In many states, professionals with senior care businesses may be required to have a license if working in their business will involve engaging in professional activities that their state regulates through licensing. It is important to remember that even if you are trained in a profession where licensing is required to practice, you may not need a license if your work activities in your business are unrelated to your profession. For example, Patricia, a personal organizer with a focus on helping seniors, actually has her doctorate in clinical psychology and practiced for several years as a clinical psychologist. While Patricia agrees that her clinical education and training help her understand her clients, she in no way engages in assessment or treatment of the behavioral symptoms of her clients. Patricia explained further to me that she typically does not disclose the fact that she is a psychologist to her clients or their family members in order to maintain expectations that her professional activities are limited to the goals and purpose of her senior organizing business. Therefore, Patricia does not need to maintain a professional license.

There are, however, some senior care business models in which the activities performed by the owner are clearly in the professional arena requiring a license. For example, Mary, a psychotherapist with a private practice specializing in aging clients and their family members, has her master's degree in social work. Given that Mary practices as a psychotherapist, her license to practice clinical social work in her state is a legal necessity for her senior care business. One final point about professional licensure is that licensure is sometimes required in order to qualify for malpractice insurance, which the senior care business owner may opt to purchase even if not all of the activities that he or she will be doing in the business are professional activities.

It is important to add that it is possible to start your senior care business while unknowingly failing to obtain the appropriate licensing. If this occurs, the business owner runs the risk of needing to pay heavy fines and penalties associated with operating an improperly licensed business.

Legal Matters

A startup entrepreneur should expect to retain and pay an attorney for assistance with incorporation. Select a law firm that specializes in startup businesses. Fees can be as high as $7,000. It might be cost-effective to negotiate an up-front package cost for this legal work. Your attorney can assist with the turnaround of documents required for incorporation, and also explain the process and check over papers prior to filing them. Keep in mind that some accountants are also quite versed in matters of incorporation and may be able to assist you along with or instead of an attorney.

Obtaining an employer identification number, or EIN, is another necessary startup step. An EIN is a federal tax identification number for a business. EIN numbers are generally required in order to operate your senior care business as a corporation or partnership. Additionally, if you anticipate that you will have employees, then an EIN will be necessary. A business owner can apply for an EIN from the Internal Revenue Service (IRS) either by phone, fax, mail, or online by logging on to the EIN section on the IRS Web site. You will need to provide a valid Social Security number. With online applications, the IRS typically attempts to validate the information submitted by the business owner and in most cases they provide an EIN immediately. The turnaround time for applications by mail is approximately four weeks. Once the EIN is received, you can begin using it immediately for most of your business needs, such as opening a bank account, applying for business licenses, and filing a tax return by mail. It can, however, take up to two weeks for the new EIN to become part of the IRS's permanent records. Follow this Internet link to learn more about why and how to obtain an EIN: www.irs.gov/businesses/small/article/0,,id=98350,00.html.

Business Checking Account

In addition to establishing your legal entity through incorporation or by forming a LLC, obtaining an EIN, and being properly licensed and insured, another important task for the startup phase of your business is to get a business checking account. A business checking account will provide you with the appearance to vendors that you are an established business. Another important benefit of obtaining a business checking account is the ease that can result for tracking business expenses, since they will exist in an account separate from your personal finances.

Take the selection of a bank seriously. If you would like to be able to easily deposit and withdraw funds from your business account using an automated teller machine (ATM), then you certainly want to choose a bank that has multiple ATM locations. If you anticipate that your business is going to involve out-of-area travel, then you may want to consider a business checking account in a larger bank with branches throughout a large region or nationwide. Another aspect for consideration is banking costs. Fees associated with a business checking account vary widely, so careful shopping is required to get an optimal business banking arrangement. There are charges for various services that you may be considering for your small business that should factor in when contemplating which bank to choose. Some banks offer business checking accounts with very low or no fees, provided that a minimum balance is maintained. If you anticipate that a minimum balance will be difficult to maintain, then offers such as these will not be relevant for your business. Some banks may require little in the way of fees for a business checking account but have relatively high fees for ATM use, particularly for use of ATM machines belonging to other banks. Therefore, if you anticipate being a frequent ATM user, then you may want to choose a bank that provides flexibility for using other banks' ATM machines. As your small business grows, you are likely going to have a need for additional banking services. Beyond a checking account, many small businesses apply for credit lines, loans—particularly for larger capital expenses—and merchant accounts. Of course, you do not have to do all of your business banking at just one bank, as other financial service institutions may have more attractive offers for other products and services.

Banks generally require specific information for opening a business checking account, including a federal tax identification number, a copy of the articles of incorporation, or a certificate of incorporation if your business is incorporated as an S or C corp. If your business is formed as an LLC, the bank may require articles of organization. Finally, your bank may also require a corporate resolution identifying the authorized signers for both S and C corporations as well as LLCs.

Marketing Materials

Thus far this chapter has addressed the essentials for getting started in your senior care businesses including incorporation, licensing, and insurance. Other basics for getting started in you senior care business include the designing and obtaining of print materials including business cards, stationery, and brochures. While many industries increasingly operate in the cyber world, where written materials are disseminated and exchanged in a digital format, the field of senior care continues to be a more traditional field where older-fashioned means of communication, such as the telephone and fax machine and face-to-face meetings, are widely used. This point underscores the need for carefully designed and attractive print materials for your business, as their use is necessary for networking, marketing, and operating your business. Attractive print materials give vendors and members of the professional community an impression that you are an established entity ready to serve clients.

One challenge with the initial printing of business materials is that it is not unusual for startup businesses to experience changes in contact information in the early phases. For example, Cindy decided that she was going to locate her senior bill-paying service in a newly renovated industrial building with cooperative office arrangements. Cindy planned to have her own office but share office equipment and reception services with other small businesses in the building. Cindy signed a lease for this arrangement and began to move furniture into her office. At that same

Business Card Checklist

- Your name
- Your job title
- The name of your business
- Your address
- Phone numbers including fax and cell phone if appropriate
- E-mail address
- Web page address (URL)
- A tagline or pithy description of your business
- Logo and/or graphic image if you have one and it fits
- List of services or products, which may be optimally placed on the reverse side of the card
- A blank line on the back of the card that can be used for writing down the date and time of an appointment planned with the card recipient

time, Cindy met with a printer who put substantial time and effort into the design for her brochure and business cards. The brochures and business cards contained the address and telephone number of her office in the renovated industrial building. The printer had suggested to Cindy that it would be most cost effective to buy a large number of business cards and brochures, as this would lower the per-unit cost. Thus the cost per card for 2,000 business cards was far cheaper than for 500. This offer made sense to Cindy. Just after Cindy took delivery of her business cards, brochures, and stationery, all bearing the address and telephone number of the office, there was a major incident in her building in which several pipes burst and a major flood occurred. Additionally, during the cleanup, state inspectors found unacceptably high levels of asbestos in the building and ordered the building closed for an indefinite period of time. Cindy was at a loss as to what to do initially, but eventually moved her senior bill-paying service into her home and made it a home-based business. Unfortunately, Cindy had to discard the printed materials. Not surprisingly, Cindy ordered a smaller amount of these materials the second time around. As this

Business Brochure Checklist

- Name of business

- Address

- Phone number

- Fax number

- E-mail address

- Web page address (URL)

- A carefully drawn or digital image that supports the theme of your business.

- Consider your audience; remember the prominent role that the client's agent plays in deciding whether to contract with your business.

- Consider the purpose of the brochure. If it's to lead readers to your Web site, then consider a small bookmark-style brochure with the business URL clearly displayed.

- Use no more than two or three fonts, and make them consistent with your cards, letterhead, and perhaps your Web site.

- The size of fonts can be congruent with the importance of the information.

- Develop a concise message and place it in easy-to-read blocks of text.

- Be clear about who benefits from your service, including the client's agent.

example suggests, it may be wise for you to order a minimal amount of brochures, letterhead, and business cards, even if it means a higher per-unit expense, as major changes are not unusual for startup businesses in the initial phase.

While it is not necessary to spend a significant sum on a graphic artist to get a fancy logo made for your business stationery, it is important to have the basics in order, such as decent card stock for your business cards and high quality paper for your brochures and letterhead. All your materials should match in terms of color or shade.

If you are undecided about a particular color, then just choose white. While it is not necessary for you to have a fully published and developed Web site, you should at minimum reserve the URL for your business, and you should place that URL on all of your printed materials. If your Web site has not been fully launched, explain to people that it will be soon. In the meantime, you should attempt to publish a very simple one-page Web site explaining who you are and what your business does, along with your contact information, at the time of your launch.

You should also be mindful that as a senior care professional you are working with a population that lived a good part of their lives at a time when life in the United States, Canada, and Europe was more austere and many people conducted themselves in a more modest fashion, avoiding self promotion. Thus, ostentatious or egocentric content on brochures and business cards may not be well received with elders or their concerned family members and agents. Consider stationery that is more understated or conservative, such as white or off-white with blue or black ink. Additionally, remember that your clients and their agents may have difficulty reading small print, so you should attempt to put all necessary content on your business card, brochure, and letterhead in as large a font as possible. Less content is more; if you can write concisely, you will be able to use larger fonts. Business cards, brochures, and letterhead should all contain the name of your business at the top and, very importantly, include the designation "Inc." or "LLC." Below the name of your business you may want to list yourself as the owner. This is particularly true if your senior care business is going to be offering a professional service, such as geriatric care management, psychotherapy, or physical therapy. Print your mailing address on all your materials as well.

Remember that if you are a home-based business, it is highly recommended that you have a post office box for a business address, and visit it regularly to collect your business mail. Using your home address can, of course, risk the possibility of an unwelcome visit to your home from a client or client's family member. This would be particularly undesirable if this individual was disgruntled. Along these lines, your business cards should contain your business phone and fax numbers, which should not be answered or used by members of your family. You may want to consider putting your cell phone number on your business cards, although it is probably not necessary to put it on brochures or letterhead. Many senior care entrepreneurs find that communication in the early phase of a case flows through the main office line, and as the case progresses, the client and professional become more acquainted and feel freer to communicate via cell phone.

As was previously mentioned, it is important that your URL appear on all three types of business materials. The importance of this will be apparent once your Web site is up and launched.

It is best to use a local printer for the printing of these materials and to avoid using online resources for printed materials, as these services often have Web sites that are difficult to navigate and may require the use of templates that may not be right for your business. You will find that the extra expense of using a local, reliable, recommended printer will be justified by personalized service and the assurance of the accuracy of the vital information in your printed materials.

You will need to have letterhead, but also plenty of matching blank stationery paper. Be mindful that as your business expands in terms of technology, it is likely that that you will create documents for which the software has created a letterhead template, so be cautious not to overbuy letterhead. You may also find that you will use more of the blank stationery that matches your letterhead than you expected. For example, many billing software programs devise letterhead for you, so when you print out a bill your business information appears at the top of each invoice.

Pricing

Most senior care businesses will bill clients privately for at least some of their services. A startup senior care entrepreneur therefore needs to know how much to charge clients for services. Pricing elder care services can follow what is customary in a local community, thus being priced in line with what similar businesses are charging for the same service. Pricing this way, however, becomes challenging for elder care businesses offering services not found anywhere else in that local community. There are, however, a few ways to deal with the challenge of establishing pricing. Senior care entrepreneurs directly providing services, such as geriatric care managers, rehabilitation therapists, or moving consultants, can consider charging clients according to how much they feel their time is worth. Direct service entrepreneurs can consider the degree of difficulty that is involved in providing the service, their amount of experience, and level of education. They can also consider the fees that are charged by other kinds of professionals who are similarly educated and experienced, such as attorneys or accountants.

Another method for yielding pricing information is to engage in what I term "stealth shopping." Stealth shopping is simply means learning about pricing in a covert way, which can involve a close friend or colleague calling other professionals or businesses doing a very similar service, either in your local community or in a community that is demographically similar to yours. By calling similar businesses and inquiring about services and pricing, the startup entrepreneur can accrue data about how much to consider charging.

Certain senior care businesses involving the owner not providing the service directly, such as home care businesses, will likely have local competition to inquire about in terms of what other competitors charge for similar services. It is best that stealth shopping not be done by the entrepreneur himself, as to avoid embarrassment and to avoid a scenario in which federal antitrust law might be broken (more about that later).

Labor Costs

Additionally, senior care businesses that hire employees, such as home care businesses, will find that they are not only competing for customers but also for employees. Therefore, it becomes important to learn what competitors are paying their workers. Obviously, an organization willing to compensate their direct care staff with a higher hourly wage may be most able to attract high-quality staff.

Startup senior care entrepreneurs will need to be able to estimate labor costs before beginning to serve clients. The total cost of labor is a metric involving the cost of service to a certain number of clients or a certain amount of hours of service. Labor costs include the wages paid to direct service employees plus the costs associated with employment, including insurance (i.e., worker's compensation, unemployment, personal injury, worker liability, and automobile riders), taxes, and advertising for the recruitment of potential employees. The cost that a senior care business encumbers to serve a client for an hour, or some other increment of time, will differ from state to state. Generally speaking, there can be a cost of 20 percent over and above the hourly wage paid to a direct care employee.

Of course, there are ways to stealth shop the cost of labor by simply having someone call other home care agencies posing as a potential employee. Wages paid by other senior care businesses can also be determined by simply asking a potential employee to reveal what the competitors are paying. A senior care business owner can ask a new employee being hired to reveal the offers that he or she has received from comparable senior care providers. Additionally, you can ask potential job candidates about their former employment experience, not only in terms of wages but also in terms of benefits and employee policies.

General and Administrative Costs

General and administrative (G & A) costs are costs associated with running your home-based senior care business, including the cost of labor. G & A costs are an important category for both businesses with employees and also businesses in which the owner is the primary provider of service.

G & A expenses capture the cost of doing business—in other words, the overhead. For the entrepreneur working alone, G & A costs will likely run the gamut, including professional memberships, travel, continuing education, marketing, car expenses, malpractice liability insurance, and communication costs including Internet and telephone services. Senior care entrepreneurs may particularly experience the cost of gasoline as a significant portion of G & A, given the amount of driving involved for visiting clients.

There is one category of expense, incurred temporarily, that some senior care entrepreneurs are willing to take on, as it is a great convenience to their clients and their agents even though it can impede cash flow. This is the establishment of a policy for forwarding funds to clients for certain necessary items, such as groceries, sanitary products, or medical supplies and equipment. Some senior care businesses will offer to purchase these items and then attach these costs onto an invoice, giving relief for long-distance relatives or other involved professionals who are too busy to purchase these items for the client. The owner of a home care business once explained to me that he felt that a great deal of goodwill and ease was created for the client and the client's agent whenever his agency was able to offer this service.

It is wise to estimate your overhead percentage even in the early startup phase. Your overhead will go up as you serve more clients, but so will your income. Solo practitioners providing service either directly to clients or by a contracted professional can expect overhead to run between 15 and 30 percent. For senior care businesses delivering services through employees, the overhead percentage will be a lot higher—more like 85 to 90 percent.

There is, of course, a relationship between the G & A of a senior care business and the fee that is charged to clients. Geriatric care managers generally report overhead expenses of between 15 and 25 percent of income received. Thus, GCMs do not typically charge as much as attorneys, who in most cases bear the cost of an office outside the home (although many seasoned GCM practices are office-based). Additionally, professionals in office-based practices typically take on the costs of more elaborate office equipment and paid employees in support roles. My own survey of attorneys practicing in my local community suggests that overhead runs between 35 and 55 percent for those who are office-based.

Supply and Demand

A consideration for the senior care entrepreneur is the notion of supply and demand. If you are providing a service that is already being done by one or more other businesses in your local community, you are in essence adding to supply. In order to attract clients to your business, you may need to offer your service at a slightly lower price, at least in the initial phase. You can certainly increase fees once you have earned the stellar reputation that you're hoping to build through excellent client service.

A strategy for acquiring a competitive advantage in a community where there are several providers providing the same service is to offer your service at a flat fee price. Flat fee pricing is a pricing structure that charges a single fee for a service regardless of usage. This can be a very strong advantage to a senior care professional in a crowded field, because it removes the potential client's fear of a prohibitively high fee given the complex array of problems in their particular case. By removing this doubt, the senior care provider with flat fee pricing may become a top choice among potential clients considering one or more providers. There is, of course, a great risk that clients may expect to have full access to your services whenever they need them. Flat fee pricing essentially works when you can, with some reasonable certainty, count on only a small percentage of your clientele actually needing substantial levels of service on an urgent basis. Another advantage to flat fee pricing is that many flat fee pricing policies require prospective (i.e., up-front) payment. Thus, the business is paid ahead of your actually providing the service, as opposed to invoicing for your services afterward and then finally receiving payment some time later.

Varying Rates

Many senior care businesses with employees who deliver direct service to clients charge varying rates depending on the time of day and the day of the week. In a policy sometimes known as shift differential, some businesses charge a slightly higher hourly rate for serving clients between the hours of 3:00 p.m. and 11:00 p.m., and an even higher rate between 11:00 p.m. and 7:00 a.m. Additionally, some senior care businesses charge higher rates for weekend and holiday service to clients. Charging higher rates for varying times can be complicated and frustrating for clients, but it also may be necessary for the senior care business to operate this way in order to find staffing for less desirable evening, overnight, and weekend shifts.

Travel Fees

Fees for travel are often charged to clients of senior care businesses, since owners and employees typically travel to their clients. There are two standard ways to charge for travel time. The first is to bill the client for mileage incurred while on duty with the client. The second method involves billing the client for the time it takes to travel to them. Billing the client for miles traveled is more typical for senior care businesses that serve clients with employees in direct care roles. The United States Internal Revenue Service's rate for reimbursable mileage amount is currently 50 cents per mile, and many senior care businesses charge that amount to their clients.

Senior care professionals who are billing directly for professional services typically bill for travel time that is somewhat extensive. In metropolitan areas where travel time is likely to involve waiting in traffic, it is customary to charge half the usual hourly fee from the time that the professional leaves his or her home-based office until the time that they reach the client. In more remote or rural areas it can be customary for the professional not to start charging half of the hourly rate for travel until they have driven for at least twenty to thirty minutes. The latter example suggests a more lenient policy for travel time in more remote areas.

Financial Management Tools

Successful management of a senior care business can include the use of specific tools. One such tool is a profit and loss statement, often referred to as a P & L statement. A P & L is a financial statement that summarizes the revenues, costs, and expenses incurred by a business during a specific period of time, such as quarter or year. Completing a P & L can show the ability of a business to generate profit

Profit and Loss Calculation

Revenue − cost of goods sold = **Gross Profit**

− operating expenses = **Operating Income**

+/− other income or expenses = **Earnings Before Taxes**

− income taxes = **Net Earnings**

Quarterly P & L figures for Chris's GCM practice:

Total revenue:	$25,400
Costs:	$6,200
Bottom line revenue:	$19,200

by increasing revenue and reducing costs. The statement of profit and loss begins with establishing the gross profit for the business and then subtracting the costs of running the business, such as operating expenses, taxes, and interest expense. Net income is then calculated by subtracting costs from revenue. Many templates for P & L statements can be found online for free. Chris, owner of a very successful private-duty home agency, explained to me that he examines a P & L statement for his business every two weeks, including each line item of revenue and expense, and compares these figures to the same line items from exactly one year prior.

Another financial management tool is a cash flow statement. This is a financial statement that shows a company's flow of cash. Funds that flow into a business are called "inflow" while funds being paid out are called "outflow." The cash flow statement breaks down operating, investing, and financing activities of the business. A cash flow statement can help determine the short-term viability of a business, especially the ability of the business to pay its bills. This is a particularly important factor for senior care businesses with payroll and payroll tax responsibilities. Cash flow statements can be helpful for displaying on paper a business's ability to cover payroll and other immediate obligations. Cash flow statements can also show potential lenders how a business might be able to repay a loan. Prospective investors can learn from a cash flow statement if a business is financially sound, while potential associates (particularly those with high-end clinical or technical backgrounds) can use a business's cash flow statement to determine if that entity has an ability to pay their fees.

The cash flow illustration for Christine's GCM practice is very basic, because she owns and operates a solo home-based business. There are more sophisticated statements available as part of accounting or practice management software programs.

Monthly Cash Flow Figures for Christine's GCM Practice

Inflow as receipts paid from client fees:	$10,300
Inflow as retainers paid for future activity:	$500
Inflow for speaker fee collected:	$400
Outflow as interest paid for equipment:	($90)
Outflow as monthly operating expenses:	($1,800)
Bottom line positive cash flow:	$9,310

07 Financial Management

Many senior care entrepreneurs have an extremely important relationship with their bankers. While some senior care entrepreneurs are able to privately fund the startup costs of their businesses or are somehow able to "bootstrap" the necessary costs with income from a second job, others need to meet with a banker, present a plan for the business, and seek a loan or credit line. If you choose to seek financing either in the startup or ongoing phase, your business plan can guide you to the proposal that you will ultimately create for that meeting with the banker. The primary purpose for obtaining a line of credit line or business loan from a bank is to ensure that ample funds are available to run the daily operations of your business, and also in order to make larger capital purchases.

Cash Budgets

One way to determine if a loan or credit line is necessary for your business and to determine how much to ask for is to create a cash budget. A cash budget pertains to the cash inflows and outflows of a business for a specific period of time. Cash budgets can be used to determine whether a business has sufficient cash to fulfill its regular operations. Creating a cash budget can also illuminate areas where too much money is going for too little return. The example of Mary, a psychotherapist with a private practice specializing in aging clients and their family members, illustrates why it is important to create a cash budget. Mary decided to create a cash budget after the first six months of being in practice. This was a fairly simple process for her as it involved simply looking at her business checkbook register, her bank statements, and statements from the one credit card that she uses for her business. Most of the business expenses and payments received and paid did not surprise her. Thankfully her psychotherapy practice was earning money. Mary did, however, notice one expenditure that she evaluated as unproductive. This was the cost of her merchant account, an account that Mary set up with her bank for the convenience of her clients. Mary thought that a merchant account that would allow her practice to accept credit card payments would be widely used by her clients. However, when Mary assessed credit card usage for her practice over the past six months, only four of her clients paid by credit card and each of them had done so only sporadically. By examining her cash budget, Mary could see that the monthly cost of her merchant account barely exceeded the fees that were paid by credit card for the last six months. Mary decided to close her merchant account, having discovered this unproductive expenditure through the process of doing a cash budget.

Large Purchases and Capital Budgets

Startup entrepreneurs will also visit with their bankers to discuss major purchases. Presenting a capital budget is a good way to illustrate that your business is able to afford a large purchase. Large purchases for small startup businesses are usually for equipment, furniture, or a Web site and stepped-up Internet presence. It is important that through your capital budget and your business plan you can attest to how a large purchase will ultimately make your business more efficient, effective, profitable, and thus valuable.

A capital budget is a process by which a business determines that a project, a piece of real estate, or a major piece of equipment is worth pursuing. The capital budget determines whether there will be a sufficient return on investment. Take for example the case of Phyllis, who owns a personal meal preparation and delivery service for seniors. Phyllis began her business with two elderly clients for whom she cooked a few times a week in her own kitchen. Soon after she began cooking for those two elders, Phyllis lost her main job in food service at a nearby university. Phyllis decided to formalize and expand her senior meal preparation and delivery service and make it a full-time home-based business. Through advertising, Phyllis went from two customers to six customers, preparing meals for each several times per week. It became clear to Phyllis that much of her home kitchen equipment was not commercial grade and was not going to hold up to the purposes of her business. Phyllis decided to create a capital budget for a commercial grade stove and oven as well as mixing equipment. The cost of this equipment was more than $7,000, but Phyllis was able to show that with the increased efficiency that this new upgraded equipment would provide, the profitability of her business would increase, and she would therefore be able to continue to draw an income and pay the loan off for these capital purchases within one year.

Billing and Accounts Receivable

Another vital part of the financial management of your home-based senior care business involves timely billing and timely receipt of accounts receivable. Deficiency with generating invoices and receiving payments will certainly lead to problems with cash flow. Getting paid is a two-way street. The home-based entrepreneur needs to develop a regular system for consistently sending out invoices, which should be stated in the service agreement that the client or client's agent signs at the commencement of service. For some senior care businesses, billing occurs weekly or perhaps twice monthly. Other professional senior care entrepreneurs choose to bill monthly, sending out an invoice for the previous month at the beginning of the following month. It is good practice to state in your service agreement or contract for services that payment of invoices is due upon the client or client's agent receiving the invoice. It is also important to have a clause explaining what happens when payments are late. Some business owners establish a policy stating termination of services if payment is not received after some period of time, while others will attach an accruing interest rate to an unpaid balance.

While Mary discovered through her cash budget that it was not worth it for her business to continue to hold a merchant account to accept credit cards, other senior care businesses do choose to accept credit cards as a way for certain clients or client agents to make more timely payments. Even though some of your income is lost in service charges and fees associated with accepting credit cards, these fees may be offset by more timely payment from clients, particularly if you have had to borrow from a credit line to offset a problem of cash flow due to slow payments from clients. Many banks offer the ability to set up a merchant account that allows your business to accept credit cards. There is typically a charge for the initial setup, as well as a charge for the credit card reader machine. If you set up a merchant account at the bank where you keep your business account, then the costs and fees associated with the merchant account can be deducted regularly from your account. As has been illustrated in a previous example concerning Mary the psychotherapist, an important consideration with obtaining and paying for a merchant account is that it is being used frequently enough by at least some of your clients that the advantage of receiving these more immediate payments outweighs the cost of maintaining the merchant account.

While receiving payment from all of your clients regularly is important for the integrity of your business and for continuity of cash flow, billing can be a burdensome process for entrepreneurs, especially when they are in dual roles of providing services and operating their business. It can be tempting for the home-based business owner to become overly reliant on payments from clients or payers from whom it is easy to collect. For example, Liam, a GCM in a solo practice, was able to establish a consultant relationship with the staff of the trust departments of two area banks. These banks wanted to have access to a senior care expert to advise them on care issues regarding some of their elderly or disabled clients for whom they were trustees. Liam worked out an arrangement for each bank to pay him a retainer of $1,200 at the beginning of the month for that month's consultant-oriented work. Liam also regularly took $700 deposits whenever he started a new case, which occurred one to two times each month on average. A very busy solo practitioner, Liam soon found that he was often financing his business, including marginally paying himself, through the $3,000 to $4,000 that he received at the start of each month from these retainers. There was no immediate pressure on Liam to invoice the clients from whom he received retainers.

Given that Liam was so busy serving his clients and could also count on a certain amount of revenue at the beginning of each month, he began to forgo billing his other clients when he had to go through the process of generating and mailing invoices to them in order to get paid. Liam woke one morning and realized that he had very little money in his bank account, and he had some clients whom he had not invoiced in nearly four months, even though his own service agreement stated that he would send invoices monthly. As a result of this problem of having no time to bill all of his clients regularly, Liam hired a woman named Linda to assist him specifically with the process of generating and sending invoices. After a few months of Linda's help, Liam's invoices went out on time, his business collections became much more regular, and his cash flow problems were solved.

The above is an example of how many senior care businesses operate in terms of accounts payable. That is, in most cases the business either requests a retainer at the beginning of service or sends out invoices and receives payment in the form of checks. An even simpler type of billing is payment on delivery. Patricia is a professional organizer specializing in organization and moving-preparation services for seniors. She charges $70 per hour for her services. Her fees are slightly lower than other organizers in her area with comparable services and experience. Patricia, however, expects payment at the end of the period of time that she works with a client on a given day. This requirement is stated in her service agreement, which is signed by the client or the client's agent. While she admits this policy is hard to maintain 100 percent of the time, in most cases she does, and her clients have come to expect that she will need a check at the end of the day. Needless to say, Patricia reports that she never experiences cash flow problems.

It is important to note that software is critical for timely and accurate billing. This becomes increasingly important as your business grows. "Wordsmithing" invoices on a word-processing document is not a viable method for invoicing in a business with more than a couple of clients. Additionally, invoicing this "old-fashioned" way is time consuming and makes maintaining and accessing client billing and payment histories laborious. It is far better to make the initial capital purchase of software, such as QuickBooks, Time Slips, Care Manager Pro, or Jewel Code, and learn the invoicing and account management features of these programs while your business is still small. Investing in the proper software will greatly enable regular accurate billing and reduce the overall burden of this sometimes tedious but all-important task.

Hiring a Bookkeeper or Accountant

One question that comes up for startup entrepreneurs is whether to hire a bookkeeper or accountant. There is not necessarily a clear answer to this question. A bookkeeper can be very helpful in setting up a system to track income and expenses that would facilitate financial analysis throughout the year and also make the process of filing taxes go nicely. However, ongoing bookkeeping services may not be necessary for the senior care entrepreneur working out of his or her home, for a very simple system that can easily be maintained by the entrepreneur is all that is needed.

Accountants are most valuable to entrepreneurs in terms of the guidance that they can give regarding taxes. However, accountants are not substitutes for lawyers, and while some accountants are lawyers, accountants are generally well versed in the rules of what can be counted as an expense and deducted from your taxes. You may already have an accountant in your life, perhaps because your spouse is self-employed or because you use an accountant for your personal income taxes. In that case it may make the most sense to simply expand your accountant's services by including his or her assistance with your business. It is probably wise to check the capability of the accounting firm if you want to hire employees at some point, as the accounting involved in hiring employees can sometimes be complex.

Bookkeeping Systems

Establishing a bookkeeping system might seem daunting to the aspiring senior care entrepreneur, particularly if he or she is a clinician at heart. Tracking the payments and expenses of your business is, however, a necessity in order to accurately pay taxes and also, perhaps more importantly, to access up-to-date information about the financial status of your business. Simple book-keeping is essentially all that is needed for a home-based senior care business, particularly in the startup phase when levels of spending and income are likely to be more predictable. With a simple bookkeeping system you are essentially concerned about income (most likely payments received for service rendered to your elderly clients) and expenditures for supplies and equipment and disbursements and fees to your employees or to professionals assisting you in your business (e.g., accountants or attorneys) or contracted assistants (e.g., virtual assistants or a Web designer). If you use your automobile for business and plan to deduct mileage as a business expense, then you will need to track your mileage.

You may choose to have more than one system for tracking certain aspects of the financials of your business. For example, you may choose to purchase software that will essentially incorporate invoice and payment information with other important aspects of your practice, such as client information and billable activity with clients. Interfacing this practice-management software with popular accounting software would provide you with a complete practice-management and accounting package and the ability to generate complete financial reports with a few keystrokes on your computer. Even if you have purchased and are using some type of business or practice-management software, you may choose to keep some type of physical ledger or accounting information on a separate piece of software. Some startup entrepreneurs can easily maintain the books on a ledger and prefer to do this for the sake of the portability of a ledger that can be taken anywhere, and also for the peace of mind that this information is not just on a computer that might fail. If you choose to keep the books of your business on a physical ledger, then I would recommend that you regularly photocopy the ledger's pages and store these backup copies either off-site from your home office (such as at your accountant's office) or store them in a fire-proof file cabinet or safe in your home. Additionally, I would recommend that you also input this information onto some type of accounting software on a regular basis. Hire someone to do this if you can't afford the time for such a mundane task.

Income

Payments to your business are the first category to be accounted for when devising your own simple ledger for bookkeeping. Payments in a senior care business are typically payments for services rendered and not for the sale of tangible products. Having said this, you may eventually plan to sell some type of product from your senior care business. In either case, payments need to be tracked. If you typically receive payments by check, essential pieces of information include the check number, who the check is from, to which account the payment is applied, and the amount of the payment. Additionally, even small businesses choose to assign an account or client number and an invoice number for every invoice generated, and thus record payments based on these numbers. Using account and invoice numbers can help avoid confusion that might occur when the payer is someone other than the client and has a different name from the client. For example, often invoices incurred by elders are remitted by the client's daughter, who may have a different married last name. Payments that do not apply to services rendered, such as funds forwarded to clients for groceries, medicine, supplies, or equipment, need to be noted as reimbursements. Failing to note these payments for funds forwarded as reimbursements might result in these payments being inadvertently counted as taxable income.

Expenses

Expenses are the other major category that needs to be accounted for in a simple bookkeeping system, and you should always keep and store receipts for expenses related to your business. All business expenses should be recorded in the ledger that you keep for your business (whether it's a physical book or a software program), and be accurately tracked by date. Managing receipts can be a nuisance given that many are received away from the office and come in inconvenient shapes and sizes. You should, however, keep them in your locked file cabinet. You might want to consider purchasing large envelopes for storing receipts. Records of your expenses should be kept in separate files according to category. For example, you can set up files for documentation of paid invoices for insurance, telephone or communications, advertising, office supplies, and postage, as well as receipts for meals. You will need to store your receipts and other documents related to business expenses for ten years, as required by the IRS in case you or your business is ever audited. Additionally, having expense-related records available from past years would be helpful to your accountant if he or she ever needed to inspect these for the purposes of completing a current tax return or revising a past tax return.

It is important to record information related to expenses in your ledger and to note the check number (if paid by check) as well as the date of the expense, a description of the expense, and the category you have decided to label that expense. It may take some time for you to be able to accurately identify what the expense categories will be for your particular senior care business. Expense categories are generally not complicated, and typically include office expenses such as supplies like paper, stationery, pens, paper clips, ink cartridges, and copy paper. In the startup phase you are likely to incur expenses in a category that you can label "capital office expenses," which could be the costs of big-ticket items such as a desk and other office furniture, filing cabinet, fax machine, and copy machine. Senior care professionals may also have a category called "continuing education," which would include the cost of books, journals, conferences, and online continuing education seminars. A large and very important category of expenses for nearly any senior care business is "communications." Communication costs typically comprise costs of Internet access, business telephone usage, cell phone usage, and advertising. Postage is an expense that is sometimes more significant than small business owners realize. This is particularly true if your business will be sending out invoices by mail, as well as brochures and business related materials, particularly when sending these in larger envelopes for which postage will be higher.

Accurately tracking the miles you drive for business purposes is necessary if you

Qualifying for IRS Home Office Deduction

Part of your home can be deducted for one of the following reasons:

- Your home is used exclusively and regularly as your principal place of business.

- Your home is a place to meet or deal with patients, clients, or customers in the normal course of your business.

- Your home does not need to be for regular and exclusive of your business and does not need to be your principal place of business as long as the use is in connection with your business.

- The amount you can deduct depends on the percentage of your home that you use for business.

- Your deduction for certain expenses will be limited if your gross income from your business is less than your total business expenses.

plan to deduct mileage on your federal income tax. For bookkeeping expenses, you can track business mileage in your ledger. Your entry can also indicate the deduction per occurrence of travel by multiplying the miles driven by the current IRS amount, which is 52 cents per mile. This amount includes the costs of fuel and wear and tear on your vehicle. You should, however, note that if you are billing your clients for mileage, then you cannot deduct that same mileage on your income taxes. You may, however, bill your clients for travel time, and if you do, you are still entitled to deduct your mileage from your Income taxes because your time is an item different than costs related to fuel and wear and tear on your automobile.

If your office is located in your home, then it is likely that you will be able to take the office deduction on your federal income taxes. In order to do so appropriately, I would recommend getting professional guidance from an accountant as to how to apportion home expenses as business expenses.

Determining the area of your home that you are using only for running your business involves calculating the percentage of the office area as a proportion of the total square feet of your home. You next add up your total rent or mortgage interest, utilities, repairs and maintenance, insurance, and property taxes for the year, and then multiply the total by the percentage you calculated above. Homeowners can also include depreciation on the business portion of the home as a business expense.

In many ways a simple bookkeeping system may seem redundant with your checking account register; however, it is important to note that you will likely not use checks to pay for all of your expenses. Therefore, the likelihood of making credit card payments, online payments using your bank account number, or automatic payments via checking or credit cards necessitates that all payment by all methods be tracked in your bookkeeping system.

Accounting Software

You may decide that you would like to have an electronic record of your expenses and income, or that you would like to have your primary accounting done on software and then have the ability to print out accounting statements when you need to have something depicting the financial health of your business in your hand. There are many accounting software products on the market. Additionally, you may find that there are some accounting software programs in a bundle of software that came with your computer. Suffice it to say that for a simple accounting system in a small home-based business, virtually any piece of accounting software should be adequate. The most that you might need to do to customize your bookkeeping software is just to create the categories of expenditures (chart of accounts) for your business. If you are planning to hire an accountant or are planning to use bookkeeping services even intermittently, you may want to verify that the accountant has ample familiarity with the software you are using. It's even better if there is a way for your accountant to input your information into their system easily so that they can do a final year-end accounting in preparation for tax filings. Intuit, maker of QuickBooks, is currently a popular accounting software program used relatively widely by accountants.

Taxes

The United States Internal Revenue Service (IRS) considers the self-employed to be people who carry on a trade or business as sole proprietors, as members of a partnership, or as limited liability companies. If you are self-employed, then taxable income flows from the income your business earns and is added to your taxable personal income, which may include income from other employment and income from your spouse if you are married and filing jointly. As a part-time self-employed person in business for yourself who owns a business as a sole proprietor or an independent contractor, you generally would consider yourself self-employed and you would file Schedule C or Schedule C-EZ with your 1040 federal income tax form.

In addition to income tax, the self-employed also need to pay self-employment tax (SE tax), which is a payment for Social Security and Medicare that would normally be withheld from the pay of most wage earners who are not self-employed. If you are self-employed, you must pay estimated taxes even if you also have a full-time or part-time job and your employer withholds taxes from your wages. Estimated tax is the method used to pay tax on income on a quarterly basis that is not withheld, as would be the case if you were employed by someone else. Failure to make quarterly payments can result in the taxpayer being required to pay a penalty for underpayment at the end of the tax year.

You'll need to complete Schedule C on your federal personal income tax form (Form 1040) to report income or loss from a business operated by a professional who is a sole proprietor or owns an LLC.

A C corporation (and also an S corporation) generally takes the same deductions as a sole proprietorship or LLC in order to determine taxable income. A C corporation can also take special deductions. A C corporation is recognized as a separate taxpaying entity from the personal owner for income tax purposes, as a corporation conducts business, generates net income or losses, pays taxes, and distributes earnings to shareholders. A single owner of a corporation pays taxes twice, as the profits from the corporation are taxed to the corporation when earned, and then this income is taxed again to the owner (or shareholders if any) when it's distributed.

S corporations can avoid the double taxation that C corporations pay. For the most part, S corporations are exempt from federal income and some other taxes (i.e., capital gains and passive income). Therefore, an S corporation's owner includes on his or her personal tax return any income, deductions, losses, and credits from the business.

A limited liability company (LLC) is a relatively new business structure allowed by state statute. LLCs are popular because, similar to a corporation, owners have limited personal liability for the debts and actions of the LLC. Other features of LLCs are more like those of a partnership, providing management flexibility and the benefit of pass-through taxation. Owners of an LLC are called members and can include individuals, corporations, other LLCs, and foreign entities. There is no maximum number of members. Most states also permit "single member" LLCs, those having only one

Requirements for Payment of Federal Taxes
Based on Business Structure

SOLE PROPRIETORSHIPS

Income tax Form 1040 and Schedule C or Schedule c-ez

Self-employment tax Schedule SE and Estimated Tax 1040-ES income tax

C OR S CORPORATIONS

Income tax, estimated tax, and employment taxes (if you have employees),which include Social Security and Medicare and income tax withholding, federal unemployment (FUTA) tax, and depositing employment taxes

You can learn more about your responsibility for paying federal income tax by exploring the IRS Web site at www.irs.gov. Canadians can learn more by logging onto www.cra.gc.ca.

owner. In the case of a one-member LLC, the IRS disregards it for the purpose of filing a federal tax return. This is only for federal tax purposes and does not change the fact that the business is legally a limited liability company, and its owner enjoys the same liability protections as does the owner of a corporation. Therefore, if the only member of the LLC is the individual owner, then the LLC income and expenses are reported on Form 1040 Schedule C, E, or F.

Most LLCs with more than one member file a partnership return, Form 1065. The U.S. Form 1065 is called a Return of Partnership, and it is used to report the income, gains, losses, deductions, and credits of a partnership and includes the owners of a C corporation as well the partners of a partnership or an LLC with multiple members.

Sales Tax

Your senior care business may need to collect state sales tax. Generally speaking, sales tax needs to be collected on most goods and some services that are delivered to a customer in the state where the business has a physical presence. It is important to note that sales tax requirements and rates vary from state to state and city to city. If a product or service that you sell or provide is subject to sales tax, then it is the responsibility of your businesses to collect sales tax and send it to your state. Most senior care businesses offer professional services that are not subject to sales taxes in most states, but it is the responsibility of the business owner to learn of this requirement in his or her locale prior to rendering a senior care service or selling a product.

Who Is the Client?

A very basic question for any professional providing personalized services is, "Who is the client?" For the attorney, the accountant, and the banker, it is a fairly easy question, as the individual client often refers himself or herself after making an initial contact with the professional. This new client then signs an agreement to receive professional services from the practitioner. The question of "Who is the client?" is somewhat more complex for many types of elder care professionals.

Some senior care professionals are hired by the elderly clients themselves. This is particularly true for senior care businesses serving older adults who are in need of some services but are not necessarily experiencing mental or physical disability. For instance, Elizabeth, an eighty-five-year-old woman who recently lost her husband, realized that it was becoming increasingly difficult for her to do her Saturday chores without him. Elizabeth's Saturday chores included going to the recycling center to drop off trash and recyclables as well as other errands such as shopping excursions for groceries and supplies. After doing some research, Elizabeth was very relieved to find that in her community there was a senior care business specializing in lending assistance with chores and errands to seniors. Elizabeth was thus fully willing and able to assess her own need, research a potential resource (the chore service), and then to make an arrangement with the business for service.

By contrast, many frail elders, particularly those with mental or emotional difficulties, may not be as capable of being resourceful, but there may be a need for help that is quite apparent to concerned friends and family. I contend that a majority of elders receiving services from senior care businesses are experiencing some type of physical and/or mental disability, and that the person who hires the senior care professional is someone close to the client, such a family member, close friend, or an involved professional such as a physician or attorney. Often, this concerned person is acting as an official agent of the elder in the role of power of attorney (POA), health care proxy (HCP), conservator, or guardian. These roles were either assigned to someone by the care recipient when he or she had no mental impairment (in the case of POA or HCP), or they were assigned by a judge in a legal proceeding after mental impairment was diagnosed (conservator or guardian). This scenario, in which a senior care service is contracted by a client's agent on behalf of the client, suggests that the senior care professional has two clients—the client's agent to whom the professional reports and by whom he or she is paid, and the client who is the care recipient.

A referral to a senior care specialist from a client's agent typically goes well when the care recipient also agrees that he or she needs that particular service. A case initiated by a client's agent gets more difficult when it is unclear the extent to which the client lacks the capacity to make a decision to consent to this service. Senior care specialists, particularly geriatric care managers, are generally well versed in working with a prospective elderly client around their consent to services, sometimes while that client's agent is emphatic that services begin as soon as possible. In some cases it is prudent for the senior care professional to do some basic mental assessment if they feel qualified and capable of doing so. If there is a lack of recent formal mental status testing, the senior care professional or their clinical associate should at least initiate a basic test to confirm that the elder has mental impairment to the extent that he or she should not be making important decisions without involvement from the agent.

A common scenario involves an elder with mental and/or physical disabilities who is gracious to the senior care professional but is unwilling to consent for services or to agree that a plan for services is needed. In some cases, a client's agent will push for a plan that may be excessive or inadequate to properly ensure the health and safety of the client. In such a case, the senior care professional is challenged to work with the client to get him or her to agree to a necessary plan of service, as it is very difficult to serve clients who are unwilling to cooperate.

Abuse, Neglect, and Exploitation

Some elder care professionals are considered mandated reporters in the states in which they work. Mandated reporter status means that they are under legal obligation to report any instances of abuse, neglect, or exploitation that they uncover in their work with older adults. Physical abuse typically means bodily harm to an elder. Neglect can include the withholding of nutrition, fluids, medicine, or proper care from an elder. Exploitation typically involves unauthorized use of an elder's funds or property, such as an automobile. Exploitation of a vulnerable elder is particularly egregious when these resources are needed for maintaining the elder in his or her home. Psychological abuse of an elder includes the perpetrator making repeated disparaging statements to an elder designed to inflict psychological distress such as anxiety, depression, and low self-esteem. Psychological abuse can also involve limiting an elder's access to friends and family members. Senior care professionals need to be acutely aware of indications that a client may be abused, neglected, or exploited and report these to the proper authority. If that senior care professional has mandated reporter status, then it is illegal for them not to report this. Abuse, neglect, and exploitation are normally reported to a public or nonprofit agency in the community that is legally mandated to investigate and address such accusations. This is quite often an Area Agency on Aging.

Perhaps one of the most difficult challenges is a situation in which a family member, friend, or involved professional turns out to have a motive not for serving the best interest of that elder, but instead to serve their own interest. For example, John, a geriatric care manager, recently told me a story from his practice when he was retained by the daughter of an elder to do an assessment of her mother's needs. During the intake with the client's daughter, the elder's daughter made it very clear that she expected that her mother would move to a nearby assisted living facility (ALF) and would thus permanently vacate her rent-controlled apartment in New York City. During the assessment with the elderly mother in the daughter's home, John asked the daughter for a period of time to speak to the elder alone and with complete privacy. He asked this primarily so he could perform an uninterrupted assessment of her mental status and to also have a more confidential discussion with her. To John's surprise, the elderly woman's mental function was essentially unimpaired. While they conversed alone, she confided to John that she feared her daughter wanted her to move out of her New York City apartment so that her granddaughter could take it over, as she had just gotten accepted to university there for graduate school. She explained further to John that she wanted to move back to her apartment and that she had the resources to get the care she needed back in New York.

John and the elderly mother agreed that he would talk very generally of his findings to the elder's daughter. When he spoke to the daughter, he mentioned that he wasn't sure her mother desired to move to the nearby ALF, and also suggested that a plan for her to return to her apartment in New York seemed feasible to him. Hours later, the daughter called John and terminated his involvement in that case. Over the next week John considered calling protective services. Just before he was to do so, however, he received a call from a GCM in New York City requesting a copy of his written assessment. This GCM explained that the elder had returned to New York and had retained the new GCM to assist with service provision. John wondered if the client's daughter, herself an attorney, feared that he might refer his concerns to protective services.

It is important to note that there are many professionals who are legally mandated reporters, including chiropractors, dentists, physicians, mental health professionals, nurses, police officers, psychologists, and social workers.

Client's Agents

Senior care professionals work relatively extensively with others who are involved with decision-making regarding an elder's plan of care, acting through an official legal role. Power of attorney (POA) is a legal mechanism that empowers the designated person to make a medical, business, or legal decision for another person if that other person becomes mentally incapacitated until the incapacitated person dies. The purpose of the POA is to ensure that the person who assigns this role has his or her wishes acknowledged. This is very important for elderly people who are facing difficult decisions around medical treatment and care, and POA documents can be worded specifically to allow for decision-making around health care.

Some states have also adopted a legal device called health care proxy (HCP). HCP functions very similarly to a POA, allowing for health care decision-making in addition to legal and financial decision-making. An HCP is more specifically geared towards medical decision-making and works similarly to the POA in that an HCP becomes effective when the person who assigned the agent begins to suffer mental incapacity. An important similarity between the HCP and POA is that the person assigns individuals to these roles at a point in life when they still have the capacity to make an informed decision on their own behalf. Therefore, the POA and HCP should never be assigned when a potential signer shows any demonstrative lack of mental capacity.

In contrast, the legal role of conservator or guardian is assigned by order of a judge through a legal proceeding. A conservator is the person appointed to be legally responsible for the management of property and money on behalf of the incapacitated person. A guardian goes a step further in that the guardian is designated by the court and is given full responsibility for managing all of the personal affairs of the incapacitated adult, including financial, legal, and medical decisions.

In summary, it is important to note that professionals who serve elderly clients will inevitably interface with other individuals in addition to the client who is the recipient of services. Most often the individuals with whom the senior care professional will interact the most will be family members. However, some clients, particularly clients with no family or estranged family, will have close relationships with more distantly related family, close friends, or involved professionals such as attorneys or trustees, and these individuals may also have legal roles such as POA, HCP, conservator, or guardian. Understanding who these players are, and knowing the extent of both their official and unofficial roles, should be a principle feature of any intake or assessment on a new case.

Antitrust Laws

There are additional ethical issues that are often confronted by senior care business owners. One such issue relates to how to startup entrepreneurs learn of certain intimate details about running their businesses, including how much to charge clients, without violating antitrust laws. While it is always best to review legal questions with your attorney, it is widely understood that professionals in a particular type of business should not discuss the fees they charge with other professionals in that same business. For instance, if you are having lunch with a fellow home care provider and a discussion arises about the fees you charge for your home care services, you might very well be in violation of United States federal antitrust law. There are alternative ways to learn about competitor pricing, such as the methods described in chapter 6.

Insurance and Documentation

Insurance

There are myriad insurance products available to small business owners, and senior care entrepreneurs will inevitably need to consider or will be mandated to purchase some of these insurance products. Most fundamentally, there is professional liability insurance. Professional liability insurance is an important insurance category for the home-based senior care professional who will be providing services directly, but also for entrepreneurs with a business model involving paid employees or professional associates acting as independent contractors. Nurses, rehabilitation therapists, clinical social workers, and psychologists all have the ability to get professional liability insurance. In some cases, the ability to get professional liability insurance is tied in with state licensing. Professional liability insurance for senior care professionals providing services directly to the clients is typically limited to that professional's activities for his or her client. Senior care businesses with nonprofessional employees providing direct care to clients may also carry or may be legally required to carry professional liability insurance for their employees when they are directly working with care recipients.

Service Agreements

A well-written service agreement is a tool that can be used by a senior care business to protect the business and its ownership from liability. The service agreement or contract should delineate important factors about the relationship between the client and the senior care business. It should also indemnify that senior care business from the actions of other service providers who may also be serving the client. This is a particularly important point for senior care businesses, as clients are often served by more than one provider as part of an overall plan of care. The service agreement should state the fee, how that fee is accrued, and the circumstances around how that fee might change. The service agreement should reserve the right to terminate services to the client and reasons why that might occur, such as the event that the desired level of service is considered to be inadequate, unsafe, or otherwise unacceptable, or for failure of the client or client's agent to remit timely payment of invoices. Billing for travel time (if any) should be spelled out in the service agreement. (See Appendix B.)

You may also want to consider briefly summarizing the process of how your business typically operates and serves clients. For example, if you begin your service with an initial meeting with the client and others, then discuss what is typically on the agenda for that first meeting and what is the usual outcome. If your senior care business offers formal written reports on findings related to assessment or client progress, then state as much in your service agreement. If you expect payment of invoices at the time that a client or client's agent receives the invoice, then state that in the service agreement and also state any penalty or extra fee levied for late payment. It is prudent to discuss required notice needed to be given by the client or client's agent for terminating services and the status of any security deposit taken for premature termination.

Release of Information

Many senior care providers have clients sign releases of information. A release of information documents that either the client or the agent (i.e., a person legally authorized to sign documents on the disabled client's behalf) allows for an exchange of information between the senior care business and other legal or health care providers or facilities and other entities.

The relatively recent passage of the Health Insurance Portability and Account-ability Act, also known as HIPAA, underscores the importance of maintaining client privacy and seeking consent to obtain or release information. While it is unlikely that a home-based senior care business would have attributes that would allow it to be considered a "covered entity" by the federal statute and thus subject to the specific mandates for compliance with HIPAA, it is important to understand that many other service providers assisting your clients are under HIPAA privacy laws. Therefore it is important to be familiar with HIPAA and to assess whether your business is a covered entity. For more information, go to www.hipaa.org.

Dual Relationships

Another ethical challenge for many senior care professionals is the problem of having a "dual relationship" within your work in a senior care case. Dual relationship simply means that you have a relationship with your client that is additional to the professional relationship. Dual relationships occur more often than professionals anticipate, and given the range of services provided by senior care businesses and the number of players involved in a senior care case, elder care professionals may need to exercise particular vigilance about this issue. Extreme examples of a dual relationship between an elder care professional and a client might involve an intimate sexual relationship with a client or someone close to the client or involve serving the relative of a former lover. Additional areas of concern include a service provider receiving monetary gain from the client or client's estate beyond the contracted amount or receiving goods or services instead of or in addition to the established fee for service. A senior care professional extending his or her relationship with a client by fostering emotional dependency for that client constitutes a dual relationship that is unfortunately not uncommon in the senior care business. Senior care professionals should always work toward promoting their clients' ability to think and act as independently as possible on their own behalf. While senior care professionals are "helpers" by nature, they should be vigilant not to confuse their personal and professional lives around their clients. This mixing of boundaries often occurs when an elder care professional engages in altruistic gestures toward the client, apart from the formal service, such as performing favors, providing nonprofessional services, or giving gifts to clients. Senior care professionals are of course community-based professionals, and there will thus be occasional and unanticipated circumstances raising the problem of dual relationship, such as social and community events, memberships in organizations, or mutual acquaintances and friends with members of a client's care circle.

An example of dual relationship is the case of Tom, who is an attorney in private practice. Christine, a geriatric care manager, had recently hired Tom to act on her behalf in a real estate transaction. As Tom and Christine got to know each other, Tom came to understand Christine's business as geriatric care manager and explained that he was having difficulty managing some of the care issues of his elderly parents. For the six weeks that Christine and her husband were in the process of purchasing their new home and Tom was acting as their real estate attorney, Christine was concurrently providing geriatric care management services to Tom's parents. While the real estate transaction worked out fine for Christine and her husband, and the care plan for Tom's parents, developed and implemented with help from Christine, was very successful, this was still a risky situation for Christine. Christine should have listened to Tom's initial explanation of the challenges that he was facing with his parents and referred Tom to another GCM.

Other examples of difficult dual relationships might involve a senior care provider providing service to more than one member of the same family. While on the surface this may seem sensible and possibly an assurance that familiarity and continuity will be maintained, it can also breed ill will if one family member feels that the senior care provider is treating another family member in a preferential way.

Objective Assessments

In addition to the problem with dual relationships, another conflict of interest for senior care providers involves objective assessment and recommendation for a plan of care that involves a particular service line provided by that senior care business. This is a particular challenge for senior care businesses that state that they provide "objective" assessment yet also engage in the provision of direct services such as home care. Thus geriatric care management firms that provide home care, and likewise home care agencies that provide geriatric care management, inevitably have to deal with this potential conflict when in the provision of GCM assessment they recommend home care as part of a service plan, or when in the provision of providing home care they recommend fee-based GCM services.

A way around this problem is to furnish the client with additional providers of the recommended service who are not affiliated with the agency. Clearly, senior care professionals need to be aware of the potential for conflict of interest in their work on all cases. Given that they are providing services in a highly interpersonal industry, senior care businesses live and breathe by relationships that are oftentimes quite complicated, and include involvement of multiple players in varying prominent roles with the client.

10 | Marketing Your Senior Care Business in Your Community

This chapter on marketing your senior care business will also discuss two other important and related activities—public relations (PR) and networking. The American Marketing Association defines marketing as "the activity, set of institutions, and processes for creating, communicating, delivering, and exchanging offerings that have value for customers, clients, partners, and society at large." The Public Relations Society of America (PRSA) suggests that "PR helps an organization and its public adapt mutually to each other." Finally, networking can be thought of as a supportive system of sharing information and services among individuals and groups having a common interest.

Public Relations Initiatives

Marketing your senior care business involves a careful strategy of public relations (PR) that may not necessarily include traditional marketing practices such as advertising in local electronic or print media. This tends to be true because many services directed at seniors tend to be too complex to communicate adequately in the traditional forums of newspaper ads or television or radio spots.

For example, Patricia, a professional organizer specializing in organization and moving preparation for seniors, was called by a sales representative for a company that owned several music and news radio stations in her local community. Patricia agreed to attend a "media conference" for area entrepreneurs sponsored by this company. While Patricia regarded this conference as essentially a three hour sales pitch by the company to have these area business owners advertise on its various radio stations, she did learn something very important about her business. The media company was offering an advertising package in which area businesses randomly advertised several times per week on the radio in fifteen-minute spots for a monthly fee. Pat considered this offer, but after attempting to draft a fifteen-minute radio spot, she realized that she could not adequately convey the purpose of her business in a clear enough fashion in that short amount of time to justify the expense of this radio advertising.

The high cost of advertising in the traditional media channels needs to be considered by the senior care professional. It is important that cost-effective methods in traditional media channels offer enough space or time to get the full message across. If this is not possible, then the senior care entrepreneur can also work to find or to create opportunities where the business can be promoted through traditional media channels for free in exchange for relaying important information that the media source is looking to disseminate.

An example of attaining a PR and marketing opportunity for free is demonstrated by the case of Liam, a GCM, and his public relations committee of the regional chapter of the National Association for Professional Geriatric Care Managers (NAPGCM). Liam's PR committee decided to do a PR initiative. This initiative had three goals. The first was to educate the general public regarding an issue that was becoming an increasing public safety concern. The second goal of this project was to raise the awareness about professional GCMs in the region. The third goal was for the committee members to educate the local community about their individual GCM practices. In order to execute this project, the committee hired a public relations consultant to design a media kit. A media kit (also referred to as press kit) typically includes a cover letter describing the organization or business and its mission, along with a press release. A press release is a relatively concise paper making a particular announcement or raising an issue. A press release includes a description of the news, issues, or problems, and whom it affects, why it occurs, and how pervasive it is. Additionally, a press release may discuss the steps involved for ameliorating the problem or how it has been resolved. Finally the press release will always state the principle informants or experts on this particular issue or problem, why they are experts, and how they can be contacted.

The PR committee of the regional chapter had decided that they were going to engage in a public relations campaign to educate the community about the increasing concern over safety and older drivers. The committee selected this issue after a discussion about recent newspaper stories about older drivers getting into serious accidents across the region. The committee then assembled a media kit, which included a cover letter introducing the issue and explaining the organization and professional geriatric care management. The media kit further contained a press release about the issue of safety and older drivers, as well as printed brochures that offered safety tips for older drivers. These brochures discussed the concerns, yet also outlined the practical challenges facing elders and why they often drive later into life than they should, and suggested constructive ways to deal with the problem beyond simply taking away the driver's licenses of older drivers with poor driving records. The brochures included information about obtaining a formal driving evaluation for elderly or disabled drivers.

The public relations committee sent these media kits out to important organizations in the region including the Visiting Nurse Association, the Alzheimer's Association, and all of the Area Agencies on Aging in the region. They also sent media kits to television, radio, and newspaper outlets throughout the region. The members of the PR committee agreed to become spokespersons for the chapter on this issue in

Example of a PR Initiative

- Phyllis decided on a PR campaign to educate her local public about the adverse health effects of seniors consuming too much sodium from fast food and from canned and frozen foods.
- Phyllis decided to assemble a media kit presenting this issue and describing her personalized senior meal preparation and delivery service.
- Phyllis wrote a press release referencing current medical research.
- Phyllis also wrote a cover letter explaining that the kit included a press release on an important senior-related topic and her business, and noted that she was willing to be interviewed on the air or in print about the issue.
- Phyllis included several business cards and brochures in the media kit as well as a biographical sketch and a photo of herself.
- Phyllis mailed these kits to local radio stations with a talk or news format, as well as to television stations and area newspapers.
- Phyllis was asked by a local radio station to appear as a guest on a health-oriented talk show.

their local markets. They contacted both radio and television outlets in their respective local areas in order to develop opportunities to discuss the problem on the air. Liam sent the media kits to several radio stations and the two major local television stations in his local area. To Liam's surprise (and dismay!) one of the television stations called Liam back immediately and said that they would like him to appear on their noon television news program. While Liam was very nervous about appearing on television, he was confident that he was well versed regarding the concerns of older drivers and was also practiced at concisely discussing his GCM business, and thought he could accomplish both in the five-minute interview. Additionally, the television reporter herself was generous enough to give a plug to Liam's geriatric care management practice and to NAPGCM.

This example underscores how Liam was able to educate the public about an important issue affecting seniors and also to promote his profession and his business at no cost. It is important to note that while this PR initiative was done by a group (the PR committee of the regional NAPGCM chapter), the process employed by the PR committee could easily be initiated by an individual senior care entrepreneur. The sidebar on page 82 depicts a public relations process employed by Phyllis, owner of a personalized senior meal preparation and delivery service.

Public Radio and Television

Senior care businesses often bill clients or a client's agent privately for services provided. This fact, and the reality that professional clients and families are in the best position to pay out of pocket for services, should guide the marketing and PR initiatives of senior care entrepreneurs. Generally speaking, public radio and public television tend to be media outlets that attract more highly educated professionals with higher incomes. While advertising (typically referred to as "sponsorship") on public radio and television can be expensive depending on the geographic area and does not allow much time for a spot, a presence in this media area may serve to raise awareness and garner a measure of goodwill with an audience with an interest in and ability to pay for senior care services that emphasize the health and safety of elders. Furthermore, the public radio and television audience tends to be more oriented toward research and being informed consumers. Given this, simply stating very generally what your senior care business is, stating its mission, and providing its Web address in a public radio or television spot may be enough to drive potential "high-end" traffic to your Web site, where potential clients can learn far more about your business.

Guerrilla Marketing

Senior care businesses face a unique challenge for engaging in PR and marketing. While the services offered and the care recipient are located near each other, the parties who are in the position to contract for services do not live in the locale of the care recipient. Given this, a senior care entrepreneur may want to consider additional PR and marketing strategies that are considered more adventurous and cutting edge.

One such "out of the box" concept of PR and marketing is guerrilla marketing. Guerrilla marketing involves the development of unique systems for promoting a product or service. It requires an entrepreneur's motivation and innovation and perhaps courage, but typically does not require a large expense. Guerrilla marketing strategies are typically unique and can be surprising to the consumer public. The goal of a guerrilla marketing campaign is for the encounter with a member of the consumer public to be memorable and to generate excitement about the product or service. The term was named and described by Jay Conrad Levinson in a 1984 book, *Guerrilla Marketing*. The term is now used widely to label unconventional marketing strategies.

Guerrilla marketing can involve unusual face-to-face encounters with the consumer public. An entrepreneur using guerrilla tactics may engage most of his or her personal and business or professional contacts and educate them on the business's services, and then explore with them various means for publicity. This process of an entrepreneur engaging with his or her network can be organized through the completion of the "Team 100" form (initially discussed in chapter 1), on which members of the business owner's personal and professional network are listed according to area of expertise (see Resources). The emphasis in guerrilla marketing is on getting publicity that is either inexpensive or free. Levinson maintains that guerrilla marketing tactics actually favor smaller businesses, as entrepreneurs with small businesses are generally more willing to be open and flexible, are able to obtain free publicity more easily than large businesses, and have closer proximity to their consumers or clients and greater knowledge about them. Levinson does, however, caution all businesses that there needs to be a real quality product or service behind any marketing campaign. Therefore, while guerrilla marketing can expand a senior care business's client base, the senior care business must also have a genuine relationship with the client based on trust, support, and an understanding of the needs of the client and the client's agent. Thus, the delivery of the service must match what is promised

- Guerrilla marketing is geared for small businesses.

- Guerrilla marketers should use a mix of tactics in a campaign.

- The entrepreneur should focus on excellence of delivering one or just a few services instead of multiple services and trying to be "all things to all people."

- Guerrilla marketing should be based on behavioral considerations of consumers and not necessarily on more conventional ideas about marketing or advertising.

- A guerrilla marketing campaign relies on an entrepreneur's motivation and imagination instead of financial capital to accomplish its goals.

- The most important measure of business success is profit and not number of sales or clients.

- The guerrilla marketer needs to focus on making new relationships on a monthly basis.

- The entrepreneur should focus on new referrals and not necessarily new clients.

- The entrepreneur should not fear or focus on competitors and instead should cooperate with other businesses.

- Use current technologies as tools for innovating your business.

in the marketing efforts. The list above is a summary of what Levinson suggests are principles underpinning guerrilla marketing. The relevance of these marketing principles to a home-based senior care business offering personalized services to clients is compelling.

It should be noted that some guerrilla marketing tactics can backfire. A memorable example of a guerrilla marketing strategy that was judged to be too "over the top" in the court of public opinion (and for law enforcement) occurred in Boston in January 2007. A guerrilla marketing tactic that confused members of the general public and law enforcement in Boston involved the placement of electronic devices throughout the city and surrounding communities, which were mistakenly identified as potentially explosive devices. These devices were in fact innocent battery-operated signs bearing the image of a cartoon character from a television show on a cable television network. The purpose of the signs was to promote the show. The result, however, was that the television broadcasting company had to pay sizable fines to the City of Boston Police Department and the United States Department of Homeland Security, and further, two of the guerrilla marketers were arrested for disorderly conduct.

Senior care entrepreneurs should thus approach unconventional marketing campaigns bearing in mind that an abrupt or "in your face" approach to marketing is likely not going to be well received by aging adults or the family members or involved professionals who are concerned for them. Having said this, there are still interesting, unconventional ways to market a senior care business. For example, Phyllis was looking to jump-start her personal meal preparation and delivery service for seniors. While she identified her clients as elders who were experiencing difficulty with meal planning, shopping, and preparation, she also knew that another facet of her market were the sons, daughters, and daughters-in-law who were concerned about the nutritional status of their elderly relatives but also were challenged to help given the busyness of their own lives. Phyllis devised a guerrilla-style marketing plan, described in the sidebar on page 86, for this potential client base for her business.

Networking

Networking is a key activity for PR and marketing. The development and expansion of your network can often stem from raising your profile in your community and online through PR efforts. Additionally, your personal and professional network can be an extremely valuable resource both for marketing ideas and for helping you in marketing your business. Basic tools for networking and for marketing your senior care business include key print materials such as business cards and brochures (even simple bookmark-style brochures) and of course a Web site. Keep business cards and brochures accessible at all times so that you have them to hand to any person with whom you are speaking about your business. Your business cards and brochures should always contain your Web sites's URL. Additionally, by keeping a supply in your briefcase you will be ready to give out multiple cards and brochures to fellow professionals when networking. Furthermore, stock the key members of your personal and professional network with your business cards and brochures. Finally, you should also develop a template e-mail that automatically places the name of your business and contact information below the valediction of any e-mail that you send, personal or business-related.

Marketing your senior care business will inevitably involve a strategy of networking with the consuming public and professionals in your local community. Networking to other professionals is a vital activity for startup senior care entrepreneurs, for two reasons. First, reaching out to professionals, including visiting some professionals repeatedly, raises general awareness of your senior care business over time. Second, clients often find a senior care business as a result of that client's family member or agent having learned about a particular business from another elder care professional. It is also important to remember that many of the members of your personal network are professionals with potential ties to referral sources or actual clients or client agents. Therefore it is important to check in with these personal network members and update them on any news about your business and keep them furnished with print materials.

Your networking plan should be well thought out and should involve regular networking activities occurring at the startup phase, but also when you are eager for more clients and when you feel that your client base is nearly at capacity. In short, you should never stop marketing your business and you should always seek networking opportunities. Networking with other professionals can be done in various settings, such as organizations of professionals and businesses in fields of aging and health. Examples of senior care providers to visit are home care agencies, retirement communities offering independent and assisted living, skilled nursing facilities, senior centers, area agencies on aging, and senior housing complexes. Additionally, physicians, while hard to access, can be particularly important, especially geriatricians or those who have a known interest in working with older patients. Specialists who often have a higher percentage of older patients include neurologists, psychiatrists, orthopedists, and gastroenterologists. Mental health providers such as psychologists, neuropsychologists, and psychotherapists who treat elderly patients can be important professionals to network with for the purpose of potentially making two-way referrals.

Other opportunities for two-way referrals include networking with legal and financial professionals such as attorneys, trustees, and accountants. Attorneys, particularly those who focus on the area of elder law, and trustees are particularly important targets for networking as they are often vital referral sources. Attorneys and trustees often have considerable influence with elders and their family members or are in an official role for the client, such as power of attorney. Additionally, traditional community-based business groups such as the chamber of commerce can offer another opportunity for casual networking supported by print materials for the consumer, such as a chamber of commerce member directory (more about the chamber of commerce below).

Public Speaking

As you become more comfortable talking about your business (this feeling often emerges once you have served a few clients), you may feel ready to speak in front of an audience about your business. Presentations can be a very effective way to market your business to both professionals and potential clients or family members or friends of clients, as a mix of consumers and professionals are often present at senior care–oriented presentations. Finding a venue for a presentation may not be as hard you think. For instance, retirement communities offering independent and assisted living options are typically interested in hosting meetings, presentations, or seminars that will bring professionals and consumers into their facilities. In some cases, these facilities may even offer to provide refreshments for the participants of your presentation.

Networking and Professional Organizations

Some organizations providing particular opportunities for networking require a fee to join; these include Business Networking International (BNI), which is a large organization of entrepreneurs providing products and services in their communities. BNI strives for its local chapters to have participating entrepreneurs in unique areas. Thus, they avoid having more than one provider of a particular product or service. BNI emphasizes the notion that disparate entrepreneurs have an ability to enhance each other's businesses by sending referrals.

Another more traditional organization with a paid membership is the chamber of commerce. Participation in the local chamber of commerce can be a very effective way for other local business owners (sometimes the real "movers and shakers" in the business community) to learn about you and your business. Additionally, chamber of commerce events are good ways to practice impromptu marketing tactics, beginning with elevator speech but also including concise but informative descriptions of your business. The chamber of commerce tends to meet monthly and also to have special events.

Another particularly effective way for senior care providers to network and promote their businesses is through an organization of senior care providers. Not all communities have organizations like this, although it would not be that difficult to form one. For example, in my local community a long-standing group of senior care professionals exists, which meets one Tuesday morning per month. The purpose of these meetings is for members to inform each other of their businesses and any changes in service offerings. Additionally, they invite speakers, some of whom are members and some of whom are not, to speak on important topics related to senior care. If there isn't a senior care organization in your community, you may want to consider starting one. A good resource for help with this might be a retirement community that offers independent or assisted living. These communities, particularly the ones that are owned by larger corporations, are often eager to get the word out about their facilities and community offerings. Thus, they often have marketing personnel who go out to the community to network and market, and may thus provide some manpower and some space for a fledgling senior care provider organization to emerge.

Social networking Web sites are also fast becoming places where entrepreneurs are able to present themselves and their businesses to the public online. Examples include Facebook (Facebook.com), MySpace (MySpace.com), LinkedIn (LinkedIn.com) and Ecademy (Ecademy.com). Each of these social networking sites, as well as the many others that exist, should be evaluated on its relative merits. For example, some maintain that Facebook and MySpace are more personal networking sites, whereas LinkedIn is more professionally oriented and used by American-based business-people, as opposed to Ecademy, which is more popular with businesspeople outside of the United States. These social networking sites can certainly serve as gateways to your business Web site and thus expand and favorably blur the line between your personal and professional contacts. A word of caution about social networking Web sites, however, is that as a rule, it is probably best not to disclose more information than you feel comfortable having your clients or client agents know about you. This is true even for the more personally oriented social networking Web sites, as there is nothing that would prevent a prospective client or client's agent searching your name and finding your social networking Web page.

It is vital to get out in the community and learn about what other providers are doing for the senior market, but also to discuss with other senior care profession-als the mission of their businesses. Getting out and learning what the community has to offer is of particular importance to senior care professionals who perform a service that requires providing referrals to other practitioners. Knowing the various entities in the community, what they do, and who the players are will orient you within the community and will give you a sense of knowledge and belonging.

Virtual Marketing of Your Senior Care Business

Online Directories

In 1991 I met a social worker before the annual conference of the National Association of Social Workers. His name was Tom. At the time of our meeting, he explained to me that he owned a successful home-based geriatric care management practice. A month later I paid for a consultation meeting with Tom, for about two hours in the basement office that he had set up for his home-based solo practice. Tom described his work life as a practitioner and entrepreneur. He discussed many aspects of working with clients and families in the role of a GCM. He also spent a fair amount of time on the business aspects of his practice. He discussed matters of billing, cash flow, and marketing. I remember Tom describing to me his view that the biggest challenge facing this emerging profession was that the individuals who typically make the initial inquiry to the GCM most often lived at a distance from both the care recipients and GCM. Thus, these emerging GCMs from the 1980s found it difficult to market their GCM practices, as it was only marginally purposeful to market locally. Tom then described how the formation of NAPGCM in 1986 had done a lot to help put together long-distance family members with geriatric care managers located near clients in need of services through the creation of a membership association with a directory of care managers nationwide.

The emergence of the Internet in the 1990s greatly helped with this challenge, as the Web site of NAPGCM now has advanced features such as a member directory on the Web site within an application called "Find a Care Manager," which enables the user to locate a geriatric care manager within a designated radius of a client using the name of the GCM, the name of the city, or a zip code. This phenomenon of a client's agent living at a distance extends to most senior care businesses. The creation of national or international associations of various senior care providers, with directories of members in different locations available to consumers, is an important way to address this problem of distance between the retainer and payer of service and the senior care service provider.

The National Private Duty Association (NPDA) considers itself the nation's first association for private duty home care providers. NPDA members provide both home health and nonmedical home care services to clients at home, and like NAPGCM, NPDA has a code of ethics that its members follow. An important feature of the NPDA Web site, which is similar to the feature on NAPGCM, is called "Find Home Care Providers." This Web page allows a user to search by company name, city and state, or zip code, and the user can specify the number of miles the agency would be from the client. These two organizations are examples of how Internet technology can optimize the concept of a member directory designed to put long-distance family members or friends together with local senior care businesses.

Web Sites

There is substantially more that a senior care business owner can do to promote his or her business in a virtual way. This mainly involves the development and design of a great Web site. An Internet presence for your senior care business is a necessity. To some extent, a business without a Web site almost does not exist, as it doesn't have a presence in the cyber world where so much business and networking occur. Rather than looking at the yellow pages or other kinds or print directories, consumers searching for services expect to find businesses on the Web by simply typing in a search term. It's becoming increasingly unlikely that potential clients or client's agents will also consult with print directories once they have identified options through an Internet search.

While it is likely that your senior care business will not be strictly Web-based, offering only services over the Internet (although some might), your senior care business will need a basic Web presence, including a Web site with a way for visitors to e-mail you. For some, the notion of building a Web site seems daunting. The reality is that it is often easy and affordable to work with a Web designer who has the technical know-how to have your site up and running in a relatively short amount of time. Unless you have had prior experience building Web sites, I would strongly suggest that you do not attempt to build your own, if you can afford not to, and instead hire an experienced and skilled Web designer. The time and effort involved for the entrepreneur who has retained a Web designer will most likely involve some initial front-end tasks having to do with writing content about the business. Once the Web designer has the needed content, then he or she can begin to build the Web site. You can find a sample proposal for entering into an arrangement with a Web designer in Appendix C.

In terms of locating a Web designer, your local chamber of commerce can be a resource, as well as other senior care colleagues. Before meeting with your Web site designer, take some time to surf on the Internet and identify Web sites, particularly in the senior care field, that are appealing to you. Pay attention to the setup in terms of colors, ease of use, and ease of contacting the organization. If you really want to impress your designer and move your project along, then for each appealing Web site, click on "Page Source," then under the "Edit" tab click "Find," then type in the word "Keywords." Keywords are terms used by search engines to connect Web sites with Web users. Copy and paste the keywords for each of the Web sites that you consider to be appealing or very closely related to the services offered by your business onto a word processing document. Passing this information on to your Web designer will give your designer an idea of the keywords that he or she should imbed in the Web site's content.

Once the Web site is launched, it will be important to have it regularly or at least intermittently optimized so that when an Internet user types search terms related to your business into a search engine such as Google, your Web site is included in the first one or two pages of results. This is a service that is sometimes done by the Web designer or his or her organization, or you might need (and might find it advantageous) to hire an additional party to optimize your Web site on a regular basis.

Having said all of the above, it is also increasingly feasible to build your own Web site. There are many inexpensive programs that you can install on your computer that will provide you with design tools and templates for creating your own Web site. Additionally, many Internet domain registrar and Web hosting companies offer the tools necessary for designing and publishing basic Web sites for little or no extra cost if you sign up for Web hosting. When planning your Web site, you should reserve at least one domain name. Given that thousands of domains are registered daily, it might be prudent to reserve your domain name even ahead of hiring your Web designer. For example, if you have decided that the name of your business will be Senior Moving Mentors, then you might think to register the domain name Seniormovingmentors .com right away before someone else takes it. Domain names tend to remain with owners for a long period of time, so if the domain name that you most want is taken, you'll have to come up with an alternative name, even if it means a new name for your startup business.

It is important for you to purchase a domain name that as much as possible duplicates or resembles the name of your senior care business. Additionally, it is particularly wise to purchase other names that are similar to the domain name that you are going to use as your URL. A URL (uniform resource locator) serves as the address on the Internet where your Web site is located. By purchasing similar domain names and having them pointed to your Web site, you will avoid users mis-typing the URL and ending up someplace else and never finding the Web site for your business.

There are multiple sources for purchasing domain names, and it is best to search around for the most cost-effective offerings, particularly if you will be looking for Web site hosting as well. Two popular sites for registering and hosting are www .godaddy.com and www.register.com. As was suggested above, identically matching the domain name with the name of your business is optimal. For example, if the name of your business is Smith Home Modifications, you may want to see if you can find the URL Smithhomemods.com. It is best to avoid URLs that are too long to be user-friendly, such as Smithhomemodifications.com. There is an appealing symmetry when the name of the business and the domain name for the business's Web site are identical or essentially the same.

One final important recommendation is to derive your e-mail address extension from the URL—for example, harry@smithhomemods.com. This will appear far more competitive than harrysmith123@aol.com. The experts suggest that when you have decided on a domain name, you should reserve it for as long a period as you can comfortably afford, as sometimes a domain name purchased for a longer period may help with a Web site's ranking on search engines. You can find resources for registering domains in Appendix E.

Beyond engaging in your own virtual PR campaign for your senior care business's Web site, you may also want to include a link to your Web site as part of your listing in your senior care organization's online membership directory. By having a link to click on that will direct the user to your Web site, the online user has the opportunity view your business the way that you would like. Having a link to your Web site and not just an e-mail address may put you at a competitive advantage because the user will be able to learn more fully about your senior care business.

Once you have chosen a Web site developer, it is important to have an understanding of the project. First there is the goal of the Web site project. For many solo home-based senior care businesses, the goal might be for the entrepreneur to be established as an accessible expert in the particular field in which he or she works. A design that is easy to navigate for the user and easy to update for the owner is also an important goal. By being able to update the Web site, the owner attains control and also does not have to pay for a webmaster to do updates. Updates to a Web site are typically changes in the description of services, such as adding new services. The owner may also update the number of years the business has been in existence or that the practitioner has been in practice. Additionally, a senior care professional may want to continue to add content over time. Since the information on your Web site is likely to be shared with professionals, clients' family members, and the clients themselves, it is important that your Web site have a clean and easy-to-read look. Additionally, it is important that the content of your Web site is easy to print.

You and your Web designer should think about the business Web site in terms of what the site will deliver. Many experts in the personal services industry attest to Web sites offering something to the user that would be useful for the problem that they are looking to solve. For example, Harry, the carpenter with the home modifications business, might want to include on his Web site a downloadable PDF form of the plans for building a wheelchair ramp. While this might sound like a self-defeating idea as Harry would essentially be "giving away the goods," it is very likely that many users will look at the plans to build a ramp and conclude that it is too complicated and decide to call Harry to build it. Therefore, including the plans on the Web site might help Harry's business to be more attractive to that user. Additionally, offering information that is regarded as helpful to the Web site visitor creates a level of goodwill that may ultimately result in a signed service agreement at a later stage.

In sitting down with your Web designer, it is important to think about the features to include. You may not want to hold back on features of the Web site if you have the time and the funds and your designer has the ability. Features that will potentially add value to the experience of the online user can include downloadable documents providing information about commonly experienced senior care problems. Additionally, it might be advantageous for the senior care entrepreneur to include voice or video podcasts on certain senior care topics. Not only will this help the visitor learn a potential solution to a senior care problem, but perhaps more importantly that visitor will get an experience of the senior care professional. I would argue that this is a particularly important feature for solo practitioners who really need to market themselves to the larger world and convey that they are sincere, confident, trustworthy, and willing to work on behalf of an elderly or disabled client.

There are other strategies that you can take to help improve your Web presence. One is to make sure that your Web site is properly linked to other sites that generally get a lot of traffic in the senior care area. Doing so will help with your rank in important search engines such as Google and Yahoo. You may want to consider paid Web-based advertising, such as Google's AdWords. Google enables businesses to purchase keywords that when typed into Google will cause the advertised entity's name and link to appear on the right side of the results page. The business owner pays whenever someone clicks on the link. The amounts can range from 10 cents to $1 per click or higher. The price determines how high up on the results page the advertisement will appear.

Blogs and Newsletters

There are other important online methods that a small business owner can use to promote and market his or her business. One way is to create a blog. A blog is a kind of Web site that is usually updated by its owner or contributors. Updates are generally regular contributions of reports of events, commentary, video, or graphics. Many blogs are news-oriented and provide related commentary in a particular subject area. Blogs are typically an amalgam of images, text, and links to other blogs, Web pages, or other related content. A blog's interactive feature, where readers can ask questions and leave comments, has particular saliency for a senior care blog where people concerned about a care recipient might be very interested in seeking a solution. Given the potential for immediacy and interactivity, a blog can be an excellent resource for a senior care business owner to present himself or herself and the business to potential clients. Moreover, a blog is not a stagnant format, unlike Web sites that change far less frequently (often due to the effort required to make Web site updates). The updating and interactivity of a blog can thus serve as an inducement for the online user to visit the blog and possibly also the Web site more often. Over time the user's positive online experience with a senior care business owner's blog and Web site may translate into actual clients.

Similar to a blog, an online newsletter can be a way for the senior care business owner to disseminate current information or commentary in a regular, ongoing format. Online newsletters can be disseminated through a sign-up feature on a senior care business's Web site. Online newsletters have some particular advantages that blogs do not have. For one, while a newsletter is "one-way communication" from the writer to his or her audience, a newsletter that is weekly or monthly allows for more careful preparation and organization. Online newsletters may also be easier for the user to print out for more focused reading later or to be shared with others, which obviously increases visibility for the Web site and business.

Newsletters can be made very simply. Typed on a Microsoft Word Pad, a newsletter should be readable on most personal computers and PDAs. Fancier newsletters may contain content written on a template with colors and graphics, including the business logo, that match the Web site. Online newsletters can be basic and can appear in the body of an e-mail or in an attached PDF document. The author of the newsletter can address the e-mail either manually, perhaps initially when the newsletter is new and subscription numbers are low, or through a special e-mailing program that distributes newsletters individually to all subscribers. Another method for disseminating an online newsletter is to e-mail a link to the Web site for subscribers to click on to read the latest newsletter. One drawback to this, however, is that not all PDA devices can easily open all links at this time.

One final advantage of an online newsletter is that the exercise of a Web site visitor signing up for your newsletter gives you the e-mail address of a person with perhaps a more significant interest, as opposed to a more passive interest, in an area of senior care related to your Web site and business. Accruing these e-mail addresses will generate a list of people perhaps interested in hearing more from you about senior care issues and the service offerings of your business. Online marketers swear by the size of subscriber lists. An important word of caution is that you should never sell or forward subscriber e-mail addresses to a third party. Assure subscribers of this policy in your sign-up policy statement. An online newsletter should probably not be considered a means to generate revenue in itself. Thus, it is not recommended that you charge for newsletters, but instead use them as a resource that adds value to the online experience of your visitors, which may lead to a transformation from occasional users to active members of your online community, ultimately leading to actual clients.

One method for jump-starting subscribers to your online newsletter is to post information about your newsletter on New-List (www.new-list.com). New-List is a Web site that serves as a directory to thousands of online newsletters broken down into various categories. Once a newsletter is signed up on New-List, a one-time e-mail will be sent to the New-List subscribers announcing and describing the newsletter with a link for subscribing to it. Information about the newsletter will then be kept in a list on New-List.

Now that your business is up and running, you may find yourself becoming capable of communicating a compelling narrative as to why your business is needed. As people learn of your senior care business idea, they may offer or ask to be a part of it. Successful entrepreneurs in the service sector will readily caution, however, that startup entrepreneurs should be particularly careful about incurring personnel costs, as these tend to be the most expensive line item in any service-based business. In addition to the cost of wages or salary, taxes, fees, and insurance associated with carrying employees, there are also legal considerations around federal and state laws designed to ensure employee safety. Overall, it may be more viable for the home-based senior care entrepreneur to contract for administrative or technical services.

Administrative Support

Administrative support contractors typically perform the functions of a secretary, administrative assistant, bookkeeper, or receptionist. Advances in virtual technology, such as e-mail, instant messages, the ability to send secure documents (i.e., PDFs), videoconferencing, and the ability for the user of a host computer to give remote access to another user, have reduced the need for business owners and support staff to work in the same office space. It is becoming increasingly common for "virtual companies" to operate simultaneously in various locations using virtual technology as a way to facilitate the collaboration. Contracting with these independent administrative support specialists is generally not difficult, but needs to be done carefully as administrative support specialists may play an ongoing role in your business.

One way to find an administrative support specialist is to explore the Internet. Many administrative support specialists advertise themselves as virtual assistants or VAs. Start with an Internet search using the term "virtual assistant." When selecting a VA you need to consider several important factors. If you are planning on having your business home-based for the long term, then having an assistant working virtually may be a particular preference. If you anticipate never needing on-site administrative support, then it is possible to contract with a VA located anywhere in the world. But what if you want the option of having your assistant occasionally work in the office? Some senior care entrepreneurs who almost always use VAs virtually also report that at times they do need their assistant to work on-site, usually for specific reasons such as projects where face-to-face collaboration is required. If you desire this option, then you should consider geographic limits when seeking a VA.

If there is no need to geographically limit a VA candidate, then consider the issue of time zones. Is there a possible advantage to contracting with a VA operating in a different time zone? For instance, it may be advantageous for a senior care professional who lives in the eastern United States to have a VA located in the western United States. With two to three hours of lead time each day for issues to emerge, the eastern United States–based senior care professional will benefit from a larger window of time to decide what tasks are to be delegated to the VA. By taking advantage of the time zone difference, the business owner and the VA can facilitate efficiency with regards to the flow of work over the course of the workday.

You also need to consider the VA's abilities and if these abilities match the needs of your business. Keep in mind that as a startup entrepreneur, you may not fully know what the business will ultimately need in terms of administrative support over time. Given this, it might be most prudent to hire a VA who has a varied skill set in both the clerical/administrative and technical areas. For example, Liam, a GCM, hired Linda specifically for the purposes of assisting him with invoicing the clients in his care management practice. Over time, however, Liam began to experience increasing needs, some of which were out of his clinical area of expertise. For instance, Liam needed to update his company's Web site and Linda possessed the skills for this. Additionally, Liam found that he was being asked to write articles and make presentations, but found himself squeezed for time to do the research necessary for these writing and speaking opportunities. Liam decided to delegate some of these research tasks to Linda, which she performed well. Over time Liam learned that Linda had far more talents than just helping with billing, and Linda became an increasingly integral part of Liam's business.

Short-Term Contractors

Not all VAs or other kinds of support specialists need to be thought of in terms of a long-term contract. Some relationships between home-based entrepreneurs and support specialists are short-term or intermittent. Many technical specialists are skilled at doing specific projects. For example, Mary, a psychotherapist specializing in aging clients and their family members, completed training in the area of life coaching. Mary intended to add life coaching as an additional service line to her existing psychotherapy practice. Mary planned to differentiate the life coaching aspect of her practice from psychotherapy by having her coaching practice be virtual, including telephone sessions, as opposed to the face-to-face sessions for her psychotherapy clients. Mary had learned from coaching course work that a virtual coaching practice requires an Internet presence and Web site with a level of innovation and sophistication beyond the basic brochure-style site she had for her psychotherapy practice, which simply described her credentials.

To fulfill this need to enhance her Web presence, Mary hired Scott, a Web site designer from several states away whom she found through an extensive Web search and then by checking Scott's references. Scott's skills were particularly desirable to Mary as he is a Web site designer who specializes in Web sites for professionals doing virtual coaching. Scott impressed Mary as a technical expert with the ability to build in enhancements and features to her existing Web site that would facilitate the coaching aspect of her practice. During his time-limited arrangement with Mary, Scott added features to her Web site, such as a blog and video podcasts, through which Mary was able to provide a concise presentation of issues that are common for her coaching clients. Along the way, Scott presented and demonstrated options for Web enhancements through online meetings with Mary, during which Scott and Mary's computers were connected and Mary spoke to Scott over the phone.

Staffing Agencies

Another way to obtain onsite administrative or technical help in your business without taking on the burden of hiring employees is to use a staffing agency. Staffing agencies are very common and are used by companies big and small that are in need of temporary help, particularly administrative or secretarial help. Additionally, many companies use staffing agencies to find needed personnel when they are going through a major transition or have a particular project that requires additional administrative support. The advantage of using a staffing agency is that while these employees work in your business, they do not work for your business, and therefore you do not bear any of the responsibilities of being an employer, such as paying for insurance or making tax payments to the state and federal government.

Reviews of staffing agencies tend to be mixed, and it is important to do some research as to which staffing agency to use. Of course, it is important to remember that if your senior care business is located in an office in your home, then the staffing agency employees will be also working in your home. It is therefore important to be crystal clear about your expectations for the arrangement of the temporary employee, and to make sure that this person has the skills and experience that you need. It may also be a good idea to get to know a little bit about the temporary employee working in your business, such as why he or she is working for a temporary agency and not working for a company. Sometimes the answer is that the employee does not want to be tied down to a job and prefers to work when he or she wishes. Other times the employee is in a transitional phase, perhaps waiting to return to school or anticipating moving out of the area. This question is important, because sometimes a short-term plan can result in less than stellar performance, particularly when the individual is anticipating moving completely out of the area or transitioning into school or a different job and thus anticipates never having to work for the staffing agency again. It's prudent to regularly check on the work that has been assigned to the temporary employee.

The rates for staffing agencies are certainly more than the rates you would pay a similarly trained and experienced employee yourself. A temporary staffing agency needs to cover the expenses of employment of their staff and also make a profit. Given this, you should expect to pay $5 to $7 per hour over what you would pay in wages to a permanent employee, while also being mindful that hiring any employee will incur additional costs, such as taxes and insurance. Hiring VAs or temporary staff from staffing agencies may be a very appropriate move for a home-based senior care entrepreneur. VAs or other types of virtual technical specialists on a short- or long-term basis can be an attractive option for short-term technical projects or a temporary uptick in the workload and resulting increased needs in administrative support.

Finding Employees

Attracting potential candidates for employment, either to hire them yourself or to contract with them, requires some thought and strategy. Word of mouth is a good way to attract skilled people, particularly if you are looking for someone that can work with you locally. It is best to get the word out that you are looking for a person with particular skills to fellow members of community business organizations, such as the chamber of commerce or other civic or professional organizations. Additionally, if you're looking to hire a technical or administrative specialist temporarily, you may want to consider calling a business similar to yours to see if they have recently had a good experience with a particular specialist. Remember that if your need can be met by a specialist virtually, you can discuss your needs with colleagues throughout the nation and the world.

Other ways to attract potential candidates to employ or contract is to look at job postings on the Internet. Large-scale job posting Web sites include Monster.com and Careerbuilder.com. Craigslist.com and other bulletin board–style Web sites are good ways to advertise for potential candidates. As a rule, it is best to ask for resumes to be attached with any e-mail reply to an online inquiry for employment or contracted work. The emergence of online resources has made it increasingly common to attract and recruit potential candidates for employment or contracted work at a much lower cost than newspaper advertising. A senior care entrepreneur recently reported to me that she typically receives a greater response from more appropriate candidates for employment by posting a job on Craigslist.com versus advertising in the "Help Wanted" section of her local newspaper. Thus, virtual communication is a very simple and low- or no-cost way to seek candidates. Through the electronic sending of resumes and references, the home-based entrepreneur can evaluate the candidate's skills and experience prior to meeting with them. One word of caution here is that you should not be surprised if you get a larger than expected response from any online ad that you place for an employee or VA. Some entrepreneurs have complained to me that managing the response from the posting of an online advertisement for employment is often time-consuming, particularly when seeking a VA with no geographic limits.

It may be advantageous to consider hiring a VA located in a lower-cost area who would thus be willing to provide service to you at a rate that is lower than what this same service might cost in your local area. For example, Henry was given the task of overseeing his local chamber of commerce's online and print newsletter. While this job had previously been done by a local printer in his northern California community, Henry thought that there was no reason why this regular printing project could not be done on a virtual basis anywhere. Henry was sure that the online portion of the chamber of commerce's newsletter could be handled virtually. When Henry advertised for this needed service online, he got many responses from technical specialists who were doing very similar projects for other organizations. In their proposals they explained that not only could they do the electronic newsletters but also the print versions. Henry paid particular attention to proposals coming from areas of the United States where the cost of doing business is cheaper. Henry's chamber of commerce finally settled on a small provider of support services based in northwestern Florida. The cost for their package of services regarding the setting up and printing of the newsletters was substantially cheaper than the local provider in Henry's California community. Therefore, by contracting with this Florida-based provider, Henry saved his chamber of commerce a substantial amount of money.

Interviewing Job Candidates

For the home-based senior care entrepreneur looking to hire an employee for his or her business, it becomes imperative to interview candidates properly, as well as to do due diligence, such as background checks and reference checks. For reasons of safety and to maintain a comfortable initial boundary, you may want to consider interviewing the best candidates for employment in some public forum and not in your home-based office. A restaurant or cafe where you can count on it being relatively quiet during some of the daytime business hours is best.

While interviewing a potential employee, pay close attention to the candidate's demeanor. Does he seem comfortable with you? Does she look you in the eye when she speaks? Does he seem overly nervous and generally uneasy? Is she somewhat nonspecific when you ask her questions regarding her experience? Negative assessments along these lines may signal that this candidate may not be particularly qualified or capable, or may not be someone that you want working in your home. You may also want to pay close attention to the clothing that the candidate wears for the interview. Clothing that is too casual or seductive may signal a candidate that may not be particularly serious or may be inclined to be manipulative or behave inappropriately. An optimal candidate is someone well dressed, perhaps even slightly overdressed, for the job for which he or she is interviewing, as this shows a level of seriousness and interest in the position.

Ask questions that will serve as invitations to allow the candidates to talk about themselves, but be careful not to probe about personal information that is not

- The candidate's height and weight if it does not relate to their ability to do the job.

- Information about the candidate's relatives.

- Information about the candidate's finances.

- The candidate's educational background if it's unrelated to the position.

- The candidate's sexuality.

- The candidate's health status.

- The candidate's marital status.

- The candidate's involvement in community organizations.

- The candidate's disabling condition if it does not relate to essential job duties.

- Whether the candidate owns or rents his or her home.

- The candidate's race, religion, or ethnicity.

- The candidate's age.

- Whether the candidate is a U.S. citizen (he or she will need to provide written proof of this prior to hiring).

- Whether the candidate has an arrest record (this information can obtained through a background check to which the candidate consents).

related to the job you are offering. It is far better for the candidates to reveal that information if they choose to do so, without being asked by you.

Listen for cues from the candidate as to whether or not they have a philosophy or lifestyle that might positively or negatively affect his or her employment with you. It is prudent to come to the interview with a relatively detailed job description for you to pass to the interviewee. Go through each of the areas and try to get an assurance from the candidate that they can actually do the job that you are asking them to do. You may also want to ask that a promising candidate do a one-day trial with you in your office, for which he or she would receive a stipend. When the candidate is working in your office that one day, be sure to give him or her a variety of tasks that you would expect the person to do in the job.

Hiring Professional Staff As Needed

Another type of hiring that senior care professionals may need to do is to hire professional staff associates on an as-needed basis. Ann, the owner of a home-based senior care agency, began to attract increasing numbers of cases. Additionally, these new cases involved aging clients with multiple and sometimes serious medical problems. Ann figured that part of what was helping her attract clients who were more medically complicated was the knowledge in the marketplace that she was a nurse. Ann welcomed these kinds of cases because, while they were challenging, she found them to be rewarding and also lucrative, as these clients typically required many hours of care each week and many of these clients were receiving 24/7 care from Ann's agency.

Ann was beginning to feel overwhelmed by the running of her home-based home care agency. She found that tending to the business aspects and the increasing clinical visits were overwhelming. She hadn't had a day off in three months when she hired Theresa, a good friend and a fellow RN. Ann did some research and devised a contract for Theresa to sign that delineated her roles and responsibilities as staff associate. The agreement required that Theresa's nursing credentials were up to date and that she carried liability insurance. Ann was clear with Theresa that she could not guarantee that her hours would always be consistent, but she felt pretty confident that she would be able to give Theresa some number of billable hours per week. Given that Theresa's experience as a nurse was somewhat similar to Ann's, Ann felt comfortable charging her clients the same rate for Theresa's visits. Ann assigned Theresa to several of the clients served by her agency and continued to charge them $60 for a nursing visit. Ann paid Theresa $40 for these thirty- to sixty-minute nursing visits and kept $20 for the general administrative cost of the agency and a little bit of profit.

Senior care business type: Personal chef/meal service

Description: Personal chefs cook at their own nearby site and deliver and set up or cook in their client's home. These chefs can customize cooking to the preferred cuisine, calorie count, amount of spicing, and timing of meals.

Relevant professional organization and Web site:

American Personal & Private Chef Association

www.personalchef.com

Senior care business type: Senior concierge services

Description: Concierge service can provide an array of services for elderly clients, including companionship, bill paying, organization of the home, errands, mail pickup and delivery, shopping for groceries and clothes, cleaning, pet care, daily check-ins, computer training and support, and house cleaning.

Relevant professional organization and Web site:

International Concierge & Errand Association (ICEA)

www.iceaweb.org

Senior care business type: Senior move manager

Description: A senior move manager works with seniors and their family members around managing aspects of a move including planning, organizing, and downsizing; packing; and assistance with settling into a new residence.

Relevant professional organization and Web site:

The National Association of Senior Move Managers (NASMM)

www.nasmm.org

Senior care business type: Geriatric care manager

Description: A professional geriatric care manager is a health and human services specialist who helps families and others caring for an aging person through conducting assessments; arranging and monitoring services; assisting with financial, legal, or medical issues; and providing crisis intervention and advocacy.

Relevant professional organization and Web site:

The National Association of Professional Geriatric Care Managers (NAPGCM)

www.caremanager.org

Senior care business type: Professional organizer for seniors

Description: Professional organizers use tested principles and expertise to enhance the lives of clients. They design custom organizing systems for their clients.

Relevant professional organization and Web site:

The National Association of Professional Organizers (NAPO)

www.napo.net

Senior care business type: Medical billing advocate for seniors

Description: Reviews medical bills for accuracy and fairness and takes corrective actions.

Relevant professional organization and Web site:

Medical Billing Advocates of America

www.billadvocates.com

Senior care business type: Private duty home care agency

Description: Private duty home care organizations provide a broad range of services, including nonmedical and medically oriented home care for elderly or disabled recipients.

Relevant professional organizations and Web sites:

The National Private Duty Association (NPDA)

www.privatedutyhomecare.org

The Private Duty Homecare Association (PDHCA)

www.pdhca.org

Appendix B:
Service Agreement Sample

(The name of your senior care business here, LLC or Inc.)

(Your tag line here.)

(Your name if you are a solo practitioner, with your degree and license or certification.)

Phone: (XXX) XXX-XXXX

Fax: (XXX) XXX-XXXX

AGREEMENT FOR SERVICES

_____, LLC, provides _____ services that typically include: _____.

While _____ strives to refer only providers of high-quality services, _____ cannot warrant and does not assume liability for the actions of facilities, third-party vendors, or private individuals hired by client(s). _____ will provide a review of all individual persons considered for hire by the client(s) for the provision of direct services. Individuals hired to provide direct services to client(s) are done so by the client(s). Client(s) assumes responsibility for payment to individual service providers and all legal responsibility related to the employment of such help.

_____ reserves the right to terminate services to a client(s) when a current or prospective care plan is judged by _____ to be inadequate, unsafe, or otherwise unacceptable and the client(s) or client(s)'s agent is unwilling or unable to accept _____'s recommendation(s) for rectifying that plan of care and authorize implementation of necessary changes.

In accordance with professional ethics and mandatory reporting laws, all professionals of _____ are obliged to report all incidences of suspected elder abuse, neglect, or financial exploitation uncovered during the provision of care management services with client(s).

The fee for _____ services is $_____ per hour. This fee is for time spent by _____ representatives on the case, including consultations with other involved professionals. Other expenses forwarded to the client will be itemized and billed. A charge of half the hourly rate of $_____ per hour will be added for each occurrence of travel beyond 30 minutes. Billing accrues in ten-minute units of time. Invoices will be sent regularly. Payment is due upon receipt.

The first direct service provided to the client(s) is typically an initial multidimensional assessment, usually conducted in the client(s)'s home or other place of residence. Following this assessment, findings and recommendations, including a potential plan of care, are discussed with the client(s) and other important persons, usually family members. A formal written report of this assessment and subsequent discussions with the client(s) or any other relevant persons is available.

The receipt of written notice served by either party can effect termination of this agreement. Should _____ terminate services, a referral to another resource will be given if possible and if desired by the client(s).

The undersigned fully understands the nature of the services provided by _____ and gives consent for such services and agrees to be responsible for payment of fees.

CLIENT NAME_____ DATE_____

ADDRESS_____ PHONE_____

RESPONSIBLE PERSON'S NAME_____

RELATIONSHIP_____

RESPONSIBILE PERSON'S SIGNATURE_____

ADDRESS_____

PHONE_____

Appendix C: Sample Proposal from a Web Site Designer*

(date)

(name)

(company name)

(street address)

(city, state, zip code)

Dear _____:

Thank you for the opportunity to revise XXX.com! As I understand, your new Web site must establish you as the accessible expert for Geriatric Care Management, while also exhibiting a design that is easy to navigate and update. The site must also include a clean, easy-to-read/easy-to-print/easy-to-download design style that appeals both to caregivers and people interested in pursuing a GCM career.

Deliverables

To support the initial requirements listed above and assist you in maximizing the impact of www.XXX.com, we need to work together as a team to ensure the following items are in place at the end of this project:

- Information structure that is easy to update and archive
- Web site design that is easy to navigate, loads quickly, and prints cleanly
- Template creation for home page, main navigation pages, and interior pages

- Population of above-mentioned pages with consistent information, including but not limited to: Acrobat-based data sheets, HTML-based information, "podcast" audio information, and shopping cart availability
- Researching appropriate background tags to heighten Google awareness
- Training to enable you to update your own pages as necessary

Engagement Phases and Schedule

To provide the above, our preliminary project plan is as follows:

Create information structure:	Complete during Week One
Information gathering:	To continue through Weeks One to Three
Review information structure:	Complete during Week Two
Design Web page prototypes:	Complete during Week Two
Create icons and graphics:	Begin during Week Two
Review and revise prototypes:	Complete during Week Three
Code prototype pages in HTML:	Begin during Week Three
Identify appropriate search terms:	Begin during Week Three
Develop "podcast" topics:	Begin during Week Three
Review HTML-coded pages:	Begin during Week Four
Populate prototypes with text:	Begin during Week Four
Research shopping-cart aspect:	Begin during Week Four
Train XX to update pages:	Complete during Week Five

Project Investment

To accomplish the tasks and provide the deliverables listed above, I estimate that your investment will be $XX.

If the work is completed with a smaller investment of my time, I will pass that savings on to you. If the work takes longer than expected because of our encountering mutually identified unknowns, I reserve the right to present a revised estimate. I will not exceed $XX without your expressed approval.

Ordinarily, I charge an administrative fee equal to 8 percent of the aforementioned fees to cover such overhead items as: casual typing and copying, faxing, telecommunications, regular postage, etc. Seeing as much of our work will be accomplished electronically, this fee is waived as the above items are unlikely to occur.

Direct project-related expenses for such items as printing, postage, mileage, etc., are additional and are billed at cost or standard labor rate. I bill on the 15th and final day of each month on a net 10-day basis. One-third of the project fee is due concurrent with the beginning of the project.

By agreeing to do work with XXX, you agree to be listed in my client list. I would also appreciate the right to discuss this project in our press releases and corporate collateral publications and materials. To give back to the community, I donate 5 percent of all net income in time or money to local philanthropic organizations.

Upon completing www.XX.com, your site will be judged as superior to the efforts of your competitors. My past work experience within the marketing realm makes me the logical choice for creating a site that will confirm your status as the expert in your field.

Sincerely yours,

_____

I agree to the terms and conditions set forth in the above contract for Web services, dated XX, 200X.

_____

President and CEO, XXX, LLC

*Used with permission and courtesy of Lynn B. Johnson, www.motormouth.com.

Appendix D: Definitions of Important Legal Roles

Definitions of important legal roles include: Health Care Proxy, Conservator, Guardian, Mandated Reporter, and Power of Attorney.

Health care proxy

A Health Care Proxy (HCP) is not to be confused with a power of attorney. An HCP is a document appointing an agent to make health care decisions in the event that the primary individual is incapable of executing such decisions. Once the document is written and signed, the primary individual continues as his or her own health care decision-maker as long as he or she is still competent to do so. HCPs are permitted in forty-nine states and the District of Columbia. HCPs are not mandatory but serve as a means for a patient's wishes to be adhered to in the event that he/she is incapable of communicating them to health care professionals.

Conservator

A conservator is a person appointed by the court to manage the financial matters of an incapacitated person. Conservators have responsibility only for the financial management of the individual and do not have any responsibility as to the care and well being of the individual and cannot make health care decisions for the elder.

Guardian

A legal guardian is a person who has the legal authority and the duty to care for the personal and property interests of another person, called a ward. Guardians are typically assigned by a judge because the ward is incapable of caring for his or her own interests due to infancy, incapacity, or disability. A guardian with responsibility for both the personal well-being and the financial interests of the ward is a general guardian. A person may also be appointed as a special guardian, having limited powers over the interests of the ward, such as regarding the administration of antipsychotic medication.

Mandated Reporter

Most states have laws that require certain service providers to report any suspected abuse of an elder or disabled person. State offices can likely furnish a list of mandatory reporters; however, these professions are almost always listed as a mandatory reporter of abuse. Mandated reporters can include doctors, nurses, and nursing home employees; psychologists and social workers; dentists; and physical therapists. Abuse of an elder or disabled person includes neglect, physical abuse, and emotional abuse.

Power of Attorney

A power of attorney (POA) is a document that allows you to appoint a person or organization to handle your affairs while you're unavailable or unable to do so. The person or organization you appoint is referred to as the "attorney-in-fact" or "agent."

General power of attorney authorizes your agent to act on your behalf in a variety of different situations.

Special power of attorney authorizes your agent to act on your behalf in specific situations only.

Health care power of attorney allows you to appoint someone to make health care decisions for you if you're incapacitated.

Durable power of attorney means that the document will remain in effect or take effect if you become mentally incompetent. The general, special, and health care powers of attorney can all be made "durable" by adding certain text to the document.

Revocation of power of attorney allows you to revoke a power of attorney document.

Appendix E: Senior Care Business Resources

General Reference

"Team 100"
www.coachville.com/basic/team100/sampleissue.html

National Association of Professional Geriatric Care Managers
www.caremanager.org/displaycommon.cfm?an=1&subarticlenbr=94

Care Management

In 2006, NAPGCM members voted to approve a new requirement that all members must hold at least one of four approved certifications. The approved certifications include Care Manager Certified (CMC), Certified Case Manager (CCM), Certified Advanced Social Worker in Case Management (C-ASWCM), and Certified Social Work Case Manager (C-SWCM).

All current and renewing care manager members must hold one of these certifications as of January 1, 2010. All new NAPGCM applicants for care manager membership must be certified beginning January 1, 2008.

Care Manager Certified

National Academy of Certified Care Managers (NACCM)
(800) 962-2260
www.naccm.net

Certified Case Manager

Commission for Case Manager Certification (CCMC)
(847) 818-0292
www.ccmcertification.org

Certified Advanced Social Worker in
Case Management/Certified Social Work Case Manager
National Association of Social Workers (NASW)
(800) 638-8799, ext. 409
www.socialworkers.org/credentials

Home Care

Certificates for home health aides—including personal care aide, homemaker, home health aide, and personal care aide—can be obtained through most if not all community colleges or any degree/technical institution. The requirements vary by state.

Also, several colleges offer a certification in geriatric care management, including online programs. These include:

Kaplan University
www.jobprofiles.org/programs/health-medical/gerontology/geriatric-care-management.htm

San Francisco State University
www.sfsu.edu/~bulletin/current/programs/geronto.htm

University of Florida
http://gcm.dcc.ufl.edu

Bill Paying Providers

www.aipb.org/certification_program.htm
www.nacpb.org/certification/cpb_ss.cfm

Medical Insurance Advocacy

education-portal.com/health_insurance_certification.html

Professional Organizing

www.certifiedprofessionalorganizers.com
www.professional-organizers.com

Move Managers

www.nasmm.org

Personal Chef Services

www.personalchef.com/acf_press_release.php

Private Pay Rehabilitation Therapy

www.nbcot.org
www.ncbtmb.org
www.asha.org

Business Plan

www.e-myth.com

Ethics

"Dual Relationship Legitimization and Client Self-Determination," Randy Johner, PhD candidate, faculty of social work, University of Regina, Regina, Saskatchewan, Canada, *Journal of Social Work Values and Ethics*, Volume 3, Number 1 (2006).

Domain Registrars

www.register.com
www.godaddy.com
www.networksolutions.com

Where to Get Your Business Questions Answered

Small Business Administration (SBA)

(800) UASK-SBA (800-827-5722)

answerdesk@sba.gov

www.sba.gov

For local offices of the SBA, check in your phone book under "U.S. Government" or visit the Web site.

The SBA is a terrific resource for business owners and potential owners, and it's free. At offices (called Small Business Development Centers or Business Information Centers) across the country, you can sign up for free training programs; receive free one-on-one counseling on everything from applying for a business license to paying taxes; and receive free publications on all aspects of starting, expanding, and operating your business. (These publications can also be downloaded from the SBA's Web site.) There are special programs for women in business, for socially and economically disadvantaged businesses, for veterans, and much more. (Two of these programs that may be especially useful are listed below.) Live online chats on all topics entrepreneurial—especially dealing with a slowing economy—are offered monthly. You can also find financial assistance in the form of individual counseling, loan application walk-throughs, and loan guaranties and disaster assistance. Did we mention that it's free?

Service Corps of Retired Executives (SCORE)

www.score.org (or contact your local office of the SBA)

SCORE, a resource partner with the SBA, is an all-volunteer nonprofit organization dedicated solely to helping small businesses succeed. Retired executives and business owners from all walks of life offer their knowledge as a community service. These folks know what they're doing, and they're dedicated to helping you. You can receive e-mail counseling or one-on-one counseling through local offices, or sign up for workshops and training. SCORE's Web site is also full of helpful information and links to every business resource you can imagine.

Office of Women's Business Ownership

owbo@sba.gov

www.onlinewbc.gov

Women business owners often face unique issues, and this organization can help you navigate your way through them all. You'll find workshops, roundtables, and one-on-one counseling opportunities to help you open, license, finance, and expand your business. The Online Women's Business Center Web site is helpful and inspiring.

Internal Revenue Service

(800) 829-1040 (for information or tax questions)

(877) 777-4778 (to reach the Taxpayer Advocate service)

www.irs.gov (click on "Businesses," then "Small Bus/Self-Employed")

Yes, we know, the idea of contacting the IRS *voluntarily* is a little intimidating. It can be done, and in fact the IRS has made good on its pledges to become a "kinder, gentler" organization. The Web site is a good place to start. You can download any form you might ever need, as well as dozens of publications. In particular, you might want to check out:

Publication 583, Starting a Business and Keeping Records (includes sample forms)

Publication 587, Business Use of Your Home

Publication 910, Guide to Free Tax Services

Publication 1546, The Taxpayer Advocate Service of the IRS

You can also request these by mail or phone.

Other Sources for Answers to Your Questions about Starting a Home-Based Business

Best Home Business Opportunities
www.gofreelance.com/home-business

Business Week Smart Answers – Starting a Home Business
www.businessweek.com/mediacenter/podcasts/smart_answers/smart_answers_01_20_09.htm

Home Based Business
www.home-based-business-world.com

Home Based Business for Women
www.wwork.com

Home Based Business Resources
www.business.gov/start/home-based

Home Business Center
www.homebusinesscenter.com

Home Business Ideas for Mothers
www.freelancemom.com

Home Business Magazine Online
www.homebusinessmag.com

Home Business Resources
www.usahomebusiness.com

Information to Start and Run a Business
www.atouchofbusiness.com

MSN Money: Top Home Businesses
http://articles.moneycentral.msn.com/Investing/Extra/TopHomeBusinessesList.aspx

North East Veterans Business Resources
www.nevbrc.org

Say Home Business
www.sayhomebusiness.com

Small Business Bible
www.smallbusinessbible.org

Starting a Home Based Business
www.home-based-business-opportunities.com/c-basics

Starting a Home Business
www.startingahomebusiness.org

Starting Your Home Based Business
www.foxbusiness.com/story/personal-finance/on-topic/small-business/help
-starting-home-based-business

The Top 10 Home Based Businesses for Women
www.selfgrowth.com/articles/Top_10_Best_Home-Based_Businesses_for_Women
_to_Run_in_2009.html

The Top 10 Home Based Business Scams
www.scambusters.org/work-at-home.html

The Top 25 Homes Based Business Ideas
www.allbusiness.com/specialty-businesses/home-based-business/3315-1.html

United States Small Business Administration
www.sba.gov

By State
Alabama: Starting a Business and Small Business Resources
www.alabama.gov/portal/secondary.jsp?page=Business_Startinga Business

Business Homepage for the State of Alaska
www.state.ak.us/local/businessHome.html

Arizona Small Business Association
www.asba.com

Arizona Business Department
http://az.gov/webapp/portal/topic.jsp?id=1158

Arkansas Business Overview
http://portal.arkansas.gov/business/Pages/default.aspx

California Small Business Services
www.pd.dgs.ca.gov/smbus/default.htm

Business in Colorado
www.colorado.gov/archive/20080527/colorado-doing-business

Colorado Metro Mart
www.cmmart.com

Connecticut Small Business Resources
www.ct.gov/sots/cwp/view.asp?A=3175&Q=391770

Delaware Business Resources
https://onestop.delaware.gov/osbrlpublic/Home.jsp

Florida Business Resources
Myflorida.com

Georgia Department of Economic Development
www.georgia.org/Pages/default.aspx

Georgia Business Resources
www.ready.ga.gov/Your-Business/Resources-in-Georgia

Hawaii Department of Business, Economic Development and Tourism
http://hawaii.gov/dbedt/business

Hawaii Community Development Authority
http://hcdaweb.org/business-resources

Business Resources for the State of Idaho
http://business.idaho.gov

Idaho Department of Commerce
http://commerce.idaho.gov/business

State of Illinois Business Portal
http://business.illinois.gov

Illinois Business and Consumer Resources
www.bcr-illinois.com

Indiana University Kelley School of Business Research Center
www.ibrc.indiana.edu

Indiana Business and Employment
www.in.gov/business.htm

Indiana Business Builder Homepage
www.indianabusinessbuilder.net

Iowa Small Business Development Center
www.iowasbdc.org

Iowa Department of Business and Economic Development
www.iowa.gov/Business_and_Economic_Development

Network Kansas
www.networkkansas.com

Kansas Business Center
www.kansas.gov/businesscenter

Kentucky Small Business Development Center
www.ksbdc.org/resources

State of Kentucky Business Resources
http://kentucky.gov/business/Pages/default.aspx

Louisiana Business Resources
www.louisiana.gov/Business

Louisiana Small Business Grants
http://usgovinfo.about.com/od/smallbusiness/a/labusiness.htm

Maine Business Resources
www.maine.gov/portal/business

Small and Home Based Business Programs (Maine)
www.umext.maine.edu/Waldo/business

Maryland Department of Business and Economic Development
www.choosemaryland.org

Central Maryland Small Business Development
www.centralmdsbdc.org

Massachusetts Department of Business Development
www.mass.gov

State of Michigan Business Guidebook
www.michigan.gov/som/0,1607,7-192-29943_31466---,00.html

Michigan Local and Small Business Resources
www.mlive.com/business

Twin Cities Business (Minnesota)
www.tcbmag.com

State of Minnesota Business Resources
www.sos.state.mn.us/home/index.asp?page=92

Mississippi Development Authority
www.mississippi.org

Mississippi State Business Resources
www.mississippi.gov/ms_sub_sub_template.jsp?Category_ID=21

Missouri Business Development Program
www.missouribusiness.net

Missouri Department of Economic Development
http://ded.mo.gov

Montana Business Resources Division
http://businessresources.mt.gov

Nebraska Department of Economic Development
www.neded.org/content/view/89/162

Starting a Nebraska Business
http://nbdc.unomaha.edu

Doing Business in Nevada
www.nv.gov/DoingBusiness_nevada.htm

Resources for New Hampshire Business
www.nh.gov/business/index.html

New Hampshire Business Resource Center
www.nheconomy.com

New Jersey Business Portal
www.state.nj.us/njbusiness/index.shtml

New Jersey Business News
www.njbiz.com

New Mexico Small Business Network
www.nmsbdc.org

New Mexico Department of Employment, Business and Economic Growth
www.newmexico.gov/business.php

New York State Small Business Development
www.nylovessmallbiz.com

New York City Entrepreneur Meet Up Group
http://entrepreneur.meetup.com/23

Business Link North Carolina
www.blnc.gov

North Carolina Business Resources
www.n-carolina.com

North Dakota Department of Commerce, Economic Development and Finance
www.business.nd.gov

North Dakota Small Business Development Center
www.ndsbdc.org/resources

Ohio Business Gateway
http://business.ohio.gov

Ohio Department of Development
www.odod.state.oh.us

Oklahoma Business Resources
www.ok.gov/section.php?sec_id=4

Oregon Local and Small Business
www.oregonlive.com/business

Oregon State Guide to Starting a Business
www.oregon.gov/menutopic/business/bus_dev_starting.shtml

Pennsylvania Open For Business
www.paopen4business.state.pa.us

Pennsylvania Small Business and Home Office Resources
www.office1000.org/Pennsylvania

Rhode Island Government Business Resources
www.ri.gov/business

South Carolina Business One Stop
www.scbos.com/default.htm

South Carolina Business Resources
www.scsea.org/resources_business.htm

South Dakota Governor's Office of Economic Development
www.sdreadytowork.com

South Dakota Small Business Development Center
www.usd.edu/sbdc

Tennessee Department of State Business Services
www.tennessee.gov/sos/bus_svc

Official Portal of Texas: Business
www.texasonline.com/portal/tol/en/bus/home

Greater Houston Partnership Business Guide
www.houston.org

The Official Business Web site for the State of Utah
www.utah.gov/business

Utah Business Resource Center
www.utah-business.com

Vermont Department of Economic Development
www.thinkvermont.com

Vermont Official State Web site Business Resources
www.vermont.gov/portal/business/index.php?id=86

Commonwealth of Virginia Business Home Page
www.virginia.gov/cmsportal3/business_4096/index.html

Virginia Department of Business Assistance
www.dba.state.va.us

State of Washington: Doing Business
http://access.wa.gov/business/index.aspx

University of Washington Business Resources from Foster Business Library
www.lib.washington.edu/business/bizweb

West Virginia Business and Industry
www.wv.gov/business/Pages/default.aspx

West Virginia Chamber of Commerce
www.wvchamber.com

Wisconsin Department of Commerce
www.commerce.state.wi.us

Wisconsin Department of Commerce: Business Development
http://commerce.state.wi.us/BD

Wyoming Business Resources
http://wyoming.gov/business.aspx

Support and Sanity for Entrepreneurs

Atlanta Entrepreneurship Center
www.atlantaeec.com

Appalachian Regional Commission Entrepreneurship Initiative
www.arc.gov/index.do?nodeId=19

Bard Center for Entrepreneurs
http://thunder1.cudenver.edu/bard

Boston Entrepreneurs' Network
www.boston-enet.org

Business Week: Entrepreneurship
www.businessweek.com/smallbiz/running_small_business

Chicagoland Entrepreneurial Center
www.chicagolandec.org

Campus Entrepreneurship
http://campusentrepreneurship.wordpress.com

CONNECT Business in San Diego
www.connect.org

Council for Entrepreneurial Development
www.cednc.org

Dallas/ Fort Worth Entrepreneur Network
www.dfwent.com

DC Entrepreneurs
http://dctechnology.ning.com/group/dcentrepreneursweb2o

Disney Entrepreneur Center
www.disneyec.com

Entrepreneur America
www.entrepreneur-america.com

Entrepreneur.com Blog: Up and Running
http://upandrunning.entrepreneur.com/2009/07/01/is-entrepreneurship-declining

Entrepreneur: Business and Small Business
www.entrepreneur.com

Entrepreneurs and Entrepreneurship
entrepreneurs.about.com

Entrepreneur Forum of Greater Philadelphia
www.efgp.org

Entrepreneur's Foundation of Central Texas
www.givetoaustin.org

Entrepreneur's Foundation of North Texas
www.efnt.org/content-about-affiliates.asp?id=35

Entrepreneur's Journey
www.entrepreneurs-journey.com

Entrepreneur Meet-up Groups
entrepreneur.meetup.com

Entrepreneur Ohio: Helping Ohio Businesses
www.entrepreneurohio.org

Entrepreneurs Organization
www.eonetwork.org/Pages/default.aspx

Entrepreneurs and Small Business Information and News
www.forbes.com/entrepreneurs

Entrepreneurship and Ethics
www.gregwatson.com

Entrepreneurship Research and Policy Network
www.ssrn.com/erpn/index.html

Entrepreneurship Worldwide
www.entrepreneurship.org

Fifty Plus Entrepreneur (Small Business Administration)
www.sba.gov/50plusentrepreneur/index.html

Finger Lakes Entrepreneur Forum
www.flef.org

Florida Virtual Entrepreneur Network
www.flvec.com

Fuel for Entrepreneurs
www-rohan.sdsu.edu/dept/emc
Global Entrepreneur Center
www.entrepreneurship.fiu.edu

Global Entrepreneurship Institute
www.gcase.org

Great Lakes Entrepreneur's Quest
http://gleq.org/gleq.nsf/index.html

Indianapolis Enterprise Center
www.indyincubator.com

International Entrepreneurship
www.internationalentrepreneurship.com

International Trade Association: Fostering Entrepreneurship Worldwide
www.entrepreneurship.gov

Iowa Entrepreneur Network
www.iowaentrepreneur.com

iVenture Entrepreneur Network
www.entrepreneur.net

Library of Congress Entrepreneur's Reference Guide
www.loc.gov/rr/business/guide/guide2

Make Your Community Entrepreneur Friendly (Georgia State Gov)
www.georgia.org/BusinessInGeorgia/SmallBusiness/EntrepreneurialCommunities
/Pages/EntrepreneurFriendly.aspx

Memphis Entrepreneurship Institute
www.memphislibrary.org/ftsbc/where/mei1.htm

Minority Business Entrepreneur Magazine Online
www.mbemag.com

MIT Entrepreneurship Center
http://entrepreneurship.mit.edu/outside_orgs.php

MSNBC Business: Entrepreneurs
www.msnbc.msn.com/id/8546545

My CEO Life
http://myceolife.com

Nebraska Entrepreneurs
http://ecedweb.unomaha.edu/entrepreneur/home.htm

Network for Teaching Entrepreneurship
www.nfte.com

Nevada's Center for Entrepreneur and Technology
www.ncet.org

New Jersey Entrepreneur
www.njentrepreneur.com

New Jersey Entrepreneur Forum
www.njef.org

New York City Entrepreneurs Organization
http://eoaccess.eonetwork.org/ny/Pages/default.aspx

Northeast Entrepreneur Fund
www.entrepreneurfund.org

Northwest Entrepreneur Network
www.nwen.org

Oregon Entrepreneurs Network
www.oen.org

Policy Dialogue on Entrepreneurship
www.publicforuminstitute.org/nde

Portland Open Source Software Entrepreneurs
www.possepdx.org

San Jose Entrepreneurial Assistance
www.sjeconomy.com/businessassistance/entrepreneurassistance.asp

SCORE Counselors to America's Small Business
www.score.org/index.html

Seattle Networking For Entrepreneurs, Investors and Venture Capitalists
www.iloveseattle.org/categories.asp?CATEGORYID=5

Small Business and Entrepreneurs
www.hispanicbusiness.com/entrepreneur

Small Business and Entrepreneurship Council
www.sbsc.org/home/index.cfm

Small Business Information for the Entrepreneur
www.inc.com

Small Business Marketing: The Wall Street Journal
http://online.wsj.com/public/page/news-small-business-marketing.html

Start Up Nation: By Entrepreneurs for Entrepreneurs
www.startupnation.com

Other Resources

The Closet Entrepreneur
http://theclosetentrepreneur.com

The Collegiate Entrepreneurs Organization
www.c-e-o.org/page.php?mode=privateview&pageID=124

The Concise Encyclopedia of Economics
www.econlib.org

The Entrepreneur's Help Page
www.tannedfeet.com

The Entrepreneur's Mind
www.benlore.com

The Entrepreneur Network
www.tenonline.org

The Indus Entrepreneurs
www.tie.org

The Kauffman Foundation: Entrepreneurship
www.kauffman.org

The Lester Center for Entrepreneurship and Innovation
http://entrepreneurship.berkeley.edu/main/index.html

The San Francisco Entrepreneur Group
www.meetup.com/changemakers

Upstate South Carolina Entrepreneur Forum
http://upstateforum.org

United States Association for Small Business and Entrepreneurship
http://usasbe.org

U.S. Senate Committee on Small Business and Entrepreneurship
http://sbc.senate.gov

Utah Entrepreneurs
www.uec.utah.edu

Western North Carolina Entrepreneur Organization
www.brecnc.com

Wisconsin Entrepreneur's Network
http://wenportal.org

Women Entrepreneurs
www.womenentrepreneur.com

Women Entrepreneurs of Baltimore
www.webinc.org

Women Entrepreneurs of Oregon
www.oregonweo.org

Young and Student Entrepreneurs
www.youngmoney.com/entrepreneur

Young Entrepreneur
www.youngentrepreneur.com/forum

Appendix G: Hiring and Firing Employees

As soon as you start hiring employees, you're subject to federal and state laws which spell out what hiring practices you must abide by. These practices range from safety standards to illegal discrimination. They are basically overwritten legalese versions of everything you should have learned in kindergarten, including play fair, show some concern for others, don't create unnecessarily dangerous situations, and being a jerk isn't in your best interest.

Some laws kick in when you have a certain number of employees, usually fifteen or more, but state laws might have different criteria and affect smaller employers. The federal laws that affect all employers include:

- The Employee Polygraph Protection Act (EPPA)
- The Fair Labor Standards Act (FLSA)
- The Occupational Safety and Health (OSH) Act
- Uniformed Services Employment and Reemployment Rights Act (USERRA)
- Whistle-Blower Protections
- The Immigration Control And Reform Act (IRCA—right to work in the USA)

Swell, you say; what do all these mean?

- Polygraph protection means, essentially, that you can't mandate an employee take a polygraph test; there are exceptions for some jobs in the security business, or in the case of suspected employee theft.
- The FLSA covers wages, including overtime and minimum wages ($7.25 an hour for 2009) and related issues (go to www.dol.gov/esa/

whd/regs/compliance/whd_fs.pdf for a wage and hour information sheet).

- The Occupational Safety and Health Act regulates, on a federal level, safe working conditions. Each state has its own safety requirements which can exceed those of OSHA.
- USERRA protects reemployment rights for those returning from a period of deployment in the uniformed services, including those called up from the reserves or National Guard, and prohibits employer discrimination based on military service or obligation.
- Whistle-blower Protections prohibit recrimination against any employee who turns you in for unsafe or unfair work practices.
- IRCA requires employers to document, within three working days, an employee's eligibility and right to work in the USA. The U.S. Department of Homeland Security has an I-9 form that all employees must submit. It verifies two facts about an employee: 1) the right to work in the US and 2) personal identity. (Go to www.uscis.gov/files/form/I-9.pdf.) You must keep these forms on file for three years after the date of hire and one year after employee termination.

Your state's Department of Labor and Industries will have information on applicable state laws for fair employment and workplace practices.

You Can Be Discriminating, but You Can't Discriminate

If the world is looked at objectively, there's no such thing as race—Just humans who, over thousands of years, adapted to different climates. The results? Different sizes, skin colors, and body features, all of which we have managed to attribute highly undeserved degrees of social importance. Thus, we classify ourselves by race, among other categories.

As an employer, you can't discriminate by race in your hiring practices. You can, and should, hire the best people you can find and leave it at that. You can make these determinations by:

- Gathering background and past job information
- Discussing the company's pricing and work policies to be sure the candidate for the job agrees with them
- Talking with the candidate to ascertain competency level

When it comes to age, you can't hire someone too young (www.youthrules.dol .gov/states.htm for state minimum age laws), and, if you have more than twenty employees, you can't, for the most part, discriminate against anyone forty years of age or older.

For All to See

Federal and state laws require you to display official labor and employment posters detailing applicable labor laws. They must be posted where employees can easily read them. These are available free of charge from your state office of Labor and Industries and from the Department of Labor (www.dol.gov/osbp/welcome.htm). For more small-business information from the Department of Labor, go to www.dol.gov/osbp/sbrefa/main.htm.

Once you've hired an employee, you should follow up with appropriate training both for the customer's sake and your own, as you don't want to send someone on a job with insufficient ability to do the job properly. Training should include:

- How to dress for the job
- Comportment on the job
- Familiarity with the products used on each job
- Scheduling and time management
- Billing and collecting payments due
- Any and all administrative work done in the field
- Promoting the company

Firing Practices

Throughout the United States, work "at-will" is the law of the land. The Employment at Will doctrine means that employment is voluntary for both employees and employers. With the exception of Montana, "at-will" allows a nongovernment employer to terminate employees who are not under contract for a specified period of time for any legal reason, or without any reason at all, at any time. It also allows an employee to leave or resign just as abruptly. This does not mean you're free to assume the crown of royalty and dismiss your employees like so many tenant farming peasants you'd like to force off the land. Arbitrary dismissal can lead to expensive discrimination claims if the dismissal is found to be wrongful or discriminatory. Various court cases have resulted in a state-by-state interpretation of the at-will relationship, so it's imperative that you understand the laws in the state in which you will be doing business.

Overall, you cannot fire an employee for:

- Discrimination based on race, color, religion, sex, age, disability, or national origin
- Filing workers' compensation claims
- Union membership
- Fulfilling jury service
- Being called up for military service
- Refusing to perform an illegal act, or, in some cases, reporting an illegal act ("whistle-blowing")

If you live in Montana, you need to be aware of the Wrongful Discharge from Employment Act, which calls for "reasonable, job-related grounds for dismissal based on a failure to perform job duties satisfactorily, disruption of the employer's operation or other legitimate business reason."

Sounds a bit ominous, doesn't it? You want to control whom you hire and let go without worrying about meeting jury duty requirements or the specifics of civil rights legislation. You can, but you'll need to establish some processes and procedures to stay legal, protect your business, and do the right thing for your employees. To prevent the wrongful discharge of an employee, consider the following:

- Know your specific state laws and local laws in regard to termination; your department of Labor and Industries can supply these and offer counsel if you have any questions. In many states you must allow employees time off to vote in elections; in twenty states, employees are paid while taking the time to vote. Other states have specific pregnancy laws that differ from the Family and Medical Leave Act, including the size of the company that's affected (far fewer than the minimum fifty employees as stated in the Family and Medical Leave Act). Inquire with your state employment office for specific laws that apply to you.

- During the hiring interview, fully explain the nature of the work expected of the employee and document this explanation, having the prospective employee sign off as understanding the demands of the job.

- Establish written company employment policies in an employee handbook, outlining everything from the number and length of breaks, including lunch during a full working day to time off for jury duty to attendance at mandatory meetings for which the employee will be paid, to weather-related and emergency closures. Explain the concept of "at-will" work and the reasons for termination. Be sure every employee gets a copy of these policies and review them from time to time during your company meetings. Note in the handbook that policies can change without prior notice, but the changes will be published and distributed. Have each employee sign off as having read and understood the handbook, and keep a copy of this in each employee's personnel file.

- Establish a grievance procedure stating how an employee can report violations to the company policies or laws, be it an anonymous or recognized reporting. Include an appeal process should an employee not agree with a management decision that affects that employee.

- Establish and publish a disciplinary process for employees whose work or conduct is not up to company expectations. The process should include oral and written warnings, progressive discipline—such as suspension or administrative leave during an investigation—fair application of the process, an opportunity for the employee to respond, and full documentation and recordkeeping of each disciplinary action.

Regardless of the applicability of any specific law, a dismissed employee can try and bring legal proceedings against you for wrongful termination. This can be time-consuming and expensive for you, so it's imperative you understand the laws, provide clear oral and written communication to your employees, and keep careful logs and records (a paper trail) of any disciplinary actions. The more open your communications with your employees, the less likely any will seek redress against you for real or imagined issues.

As long as you aren't violating the law, you can dismiss an employee, even if your reasoning seems arbitrary. You simply have to be sure your reasoning can't be shown to look too much like a violation of a legal protection. One exception to this type of dismissal is if you and your employee signed a contract that covered a specific period of time. In that case, you can't terminate without good cause unless the contract has a clause stating either party can end the agreement without any consequence.

Your employees have some responsibilities, too. They must take all required breaks during the work day at the normal times; they cannot bank these times and leave early or come in late. Some exceptions can be made when the nature of the work prevents taking a break. Check with your state's Department of Labor and Industries for specific guidelines.

Holidays

You don't *have* to stop working on any holidays, but you'll find yourself working alone if you don't recognize at least some of the following ten national holidays:

- New Year's Day
- Martin Luther King Junior's Birthday
- Washington's Birthday or Presidents Day
- Memorial Day
- Independence Day
- Labor Day
- Columbus Day
- Veterans Day
- Thanksgiving Day
- Christmas Day

You only have to pay your regular hourly rate for holiday work unless working a holiday exceeds a forty-hour week. You don't have to give paid holiday leave, either, should you choose to close down for any given holiday. Many companies traditionally offer some paid holidays, however. You don't have to offer paid vacations, either, although if you want to remain competitive and attract good employees, you'll most likely offer some kind of package that includes holidays off, some with pay, and paid vacation days. These benefits are strictly a matter of negotiation between you and your employees. The law doesn't force you to provide paid holidays, days off, vacations, or sick days. But good business sense will take you in this direction.

Appendix H:
Tax Issues

Reducing Your Taxes with Deductions

There are plenty of legitimate tax deductions available to you:

- Office overhead and expenses (everything from your telephone costs to office supplies to the purchase of a desk)
- All the supplies and materials used in the course of your work
- Your automobile expenses as they relate to your work. For instance, you can deduct the cost of driving to and from clients, picking up supplies, or giving estimates. Any personal use of the vehicle during non-work hours is not deductible.
- All employee-related costs, including wages, training, and paid benefits
- Professional services (legal and accounting, for instance, including tax preparation)
- Repairs and maintenance.
- Rent on office or storage space
- Insurance
- License and bond
- One-half of your FICA or self-employment tax

Office Deduction

Deducting your *physical home office*, as opposed to deducting office expenses, raises a red flag with the IRS. You can always deduct any business-related office expenses, such as your phone, computer, paper, and so on. You can also deduct the physical space itself, if you meet IRS requirements. These deductions can include a percentage of utility bills, mortgage interest, repairs, and depreciation, and are reported on IRS *Form 8829, Expenses for Business Use of Your Home*. You'll find this inside *Publication 587, Business Use of Your Home*, which will help you determine if your home office meets the IRS requirements.

What are the IRS requirements? Your home office:

1. must be used exclusively and regularly for business, including administrative and management activities which are not primarily conducted elsewhere; and
2. it must be your principal place of business, or be used to meet with clients or customers during the normal course of business.

If you have a separate structure, such as a detached cottage, it's much easier to meet the home office deduction requirements. A structure or space that's used for storage or repair work is also a viable deduction. As most of your time will be spent outside the office, and therefore little of your business will be done in the office, it will be tough to justify the deduction.

Employees

If you have employees when you start up your business, or expect to have them later, here are some things you need to know regarding taxes and recordkeeping:

- Keep track of hours and dates worked.
- Deduct and account for all federal and state taxes per pay period.
- Deduct and account for any voluntary payroll deductions, including health insurance premiums and retirement plan contributions.

Tax deductions include:

- Federal income tax withholding (see IRS Publication 15)
- Federal Insurance Contributions Act (FICA) withholding—6.2 percent by the employer and 6.2 percent by the employee
- Medicare withholding (1.45 percent of wages paid by the employer and 1.45 percent by the employee)
- Federal unemployment taxes (FUTA)
- State unemployment taxes (SUTA)
- State income tax withholding (if applicable)
- Any local tax withholdings (city, county, state disability, etc.)

As the employer, you must collect all these taxes, record them, be sure they reconcile with the employees' salary and working hours, and then send the taxes along to the appropriate government agency while filing all payroll tax returns.

To file the returns, you will use the following forms:

- *Form 940* or *Form 940EZ* for annual federal unemployment taxes
- *Form 941*, the employer's quarterly payroll tax return
- *Form 945, Annual Return of Withheld Federal Income Tax*
- *Wage and Tax Statements* or *W-2*
- *Form 8109, Federal Tax Deposit Coupon* (accompanies *Form 941*)
- Appropriate state and local tax forms

All of these forms are available at your state treasurer's office and from the IRS, at www.irs.gov.

Estimated Tax Worksheet

As you earn money, you must set some aside for taxes. If you anticipate owing more than $1,000 in taxes by the end of the year, you must make quarterly payments to Uncle Sam. These four payments are due the fifteenth of January, April, June, and September. Use IRS form 1040-ES to help calculate the amount you owe. You will also use this form to submit your payment to the government.

2009 Estimated Tax Worksheet

Keep for Your Records

1	Adjusted gross income you expect in 2009 (see instructions below)	**1**	
2	• If you plan to itemize deductions, enter the estimated total of your itemized deductions. **Caution:** *If line 1 above is over $166,800 ($83,400 if married filing separately), your deduction may be reduced. See Pub. 505 for details.* • If you do not plan to itemize deductions, enter your standard deduction from page 1 or Pub. 505, Worksheet 2-3.	**2**	
3	Subtract line 2 from line 1	**3**	
4	Exemptions. Multiply $3,650 by the number of personal exemptions. **Caution:** *See Pub. 505 to figure the amount to enter if line 1 above is over: $250,200 if married filing jointly or qualifying widow(er); $208,500 if head of household; $166,800 if single; or $125,100 if married filing separately*	**4**	
5	Subtract line 4 from line 3	**5**	
6	Tax. Figure your tax on the amount on line 5 by using the **2009 Tax Rate Schedules** on page 5. **Caution:** *If you will have qualified dividends or a net capital gain, or expect to claim the foreign earned income exclusion or housing exclusion, see Pub. 505 to figure the tax*	**6**	
7	Alternative minimum tax from **Form 6251**	**7**	
8	Add lines 6 and 7. Add to this amount any other taxes you expect to include in the total on Form 1040, line 44, or Form 1040A, line 28	**8**	
9	Credits (see instructions below). **Do not** include any income tax withholding on this line	**9**	
10	Subtract line 9 from line 8. If zero or less, enter -0-	**10**	
11	Self-employment tax (see instructions below). Estimate of 2009 net earnings from self-employment $_____ ; if **$106,800 or less,** multiply the amount by 15.3%; if **more than $106,800,** multiply the amount by 2.9%, add $13,243.20 to the result, and enter the total. **Caution:** *If you also have wages subject to social security tax or the 6.2% portion of tier 1 Railroad Retirement tax, see Pub. 505 to figure the amount to enter*	**11**	
12	Other taxes (see instructions below)	**12**	
13a	Add lines 10 through 12	**13a**	
b	Earned income credit, additional child tax credit, and credits from **Forms 4136, 5405, 8801 (line 27),** and **8885**	**13b**	
c	**Total 2009 estimated tax.** Subtract line 13b from line 13a. If zero or less, enter -0- . . . . . ▶	**13c**	

14a	Multiply line 13c by 90% (66⅔ % for farmers and fishermen)	**14a**		
b	Enter the tax shown on your 2008 tax return (110% of that amount if you are not a farmer or fisherman and the adjusted gross income shown on that return is more than $150,000 or, if married filing separately for 2009, more than $75,000)	**14b**		
c	**Required annual payment to avoid a penalty.** Enter the **smaller** of line 14a or 14b . . . . . ▶		**14c**	

Caution: *Generally, if you do not prepay (through income tax withholding and estimated tax payments) at least the amount on line 14c, you may owe a penalty for not paying enough estimated tax. To avoid a penalty, make sure your estimate on line 13c is as accurate as possible. Even if you pay the required annual payment, you may still owe tax when you file your return. If you prefer, you can pay the amount shown on line 13c. For details, see Pub. 505.*

15	Income tax withheld and estimated to be withheld during 2009 (including income tax withholding on pensions, annuities, certain deferred income, etc.)	**15**	
16a	Subtract line 15 from line 14c	**16a**	

Is the result zero or less?

☐ **Yes.** Stop here. You are not required to make estimated tax payments.

☐ **No.** Go to line 16b.

b	Subtract line 15 from line 13c	**16b**	

Is the result less than $1,000?

☐ **Yes.** Stop here. You are not required to make estimated tax payments.

☐ **No.** Go to line 17 to figure your required payment.

17	If the first payment you are required to make is due April 15, 2009, enter ¼ of line 16a (minus any 2008 overpayment that you are applying to this installment) here, and on your estimated tax payment voucher(s) if you are paying by check or money order. (**Note:** *Household employers, see instructions below.*)	**17**	

Instructions for the 2009 Estimated Tax Worksheet

Line 1. Adjusted gross income. Use your 2008 tax return and instructions as a guide to figuring the adjusted gross income you expect in 2009 (but be sure to consider the items listed under *What's New* that begins on page 1). For more details on figuring your adjusted gross income, see *Expected AGI—Line 1* in chapter 2 of Pub. 505. If you are self-employed, be sure to take into account the deduction for one-half of your self-employment tax (2008 Form 1040, line 27).

Line 9. Credits. See the 2008 Form 1040, lines 47 through 54, or Form 1040A, lines 29 through 33, and the related instructions.

Line 11. Self-employment tax. If you and your spouse make joint estimated tax payments and you both have self-employment income, figure the self-employment tax for each of you separately. Enter the total on line 11. When figuring your estimate of 2009 net earnings from self-employment, be sure to use only 92.35% (.9235) of your total net profit from self-employment.

Line 12. Other taxes. Use the instructions for the 2008 Form 1040 to determine if you expect to owe, for 2009, any of the taxes that would have been entered on your 2008 Form 1040, lines 59 (additional tax on early distributions only) and 60, and any write-ins on line 61, or any amount from Form 1040A, line 36. On line 12, enter the total of those taxes, subject to the following two exceptions.

Exception 1. Include household employment taxes from box b of Form 1040, line 60, on this line only if:

• You will have federal income tax withheld from wages, pensions, annuities, gambling winnings, or other income, or

• You would be required to make estimated tax payments (to avoid a penalty) even if you did not include household employment taxes when figuring your estimated tax.

If you meet one or both of the above, include in the amount on line 12 the total of your household employment taxes before subtracting advance EIC payments made to your employee(s).

Exception 2. Of the amounts for other taxes that may be entered on Form 1040, line 61, do not include on line 12: tax on recapture of a federal mortgage subsidy, uncollected employee social security and Medicare tax or RRTA tax on tips or group-term life insurance, tax on golden parachute payments, look-back interest due under section 167(g) or 460(b), or excise tax on insider stock compensation from an expatriated corporation. These taxes are not required to be paid until the due date of your income tax return (not including extensions).

Repayment of first-time homebuyer credit. If you claimed the first-time homebuyer credit for 2008 and the home ceased to be your main home in 2009, you generally must include on line 12 the entire credit you claimed for 2008. This includes situations where you sell the home or convert it to business or rental property. See Form 5405 for exceptions.

Line 17. If you are a household employer and you make advance EIC payments to your employee(s), reduce your required estimated tax payment for each period by the amount of advance EIC payments paid during the period.

Index

About the Author

After earning his master's degree in social work from Rutgers University, James Ferry began his professional career as a social worker and discharge planner in a physical rehabilitation hospital, working with many families struggling in crisis when their aging family members experienced life-changing illnesses or injuries. Finding that many caregivers become overwhelmed by the stress and strain of managing the changes resulting from medical crises, particularly caregivers who live far away and have families and jobs of their own, in 1992 he began working in geriatric care management. In 2003 he established Coaching Caregivers, LLC, a geriatric care management, coaching, and consulting firm in Deerfield, Massachusetts (www.coachingcaregivers.com).

Coaching Caregivers, LLC, offers solutions and support to busy adults who have caregiving responsibilities. Coaching Caregivers, LLC, also provides programs, products, and services to caregivers who live and work across the nation. Ferry particularly enjoys sharing solutions with those who have the desire to begin or resume personal and professional achievement, outside their role as caregiver.

Ferry currently is a PhD candidate in social work at the University at Albany and has coauthored several articles on geriatric care management that have appeared in the journals *Compensation and Benefits Management, Journal of Medical Practice Management,* and *Inside Case Management.* Additionally, he is first author of "Toward an Understanding of the Clinical Aspects of Geriatric Case Management," published in the spring 2006 edition of the journal *Social Work in Health Care.*

Ferry also provides coaching and mentorship to aspiring or established senior care professionals interested in small business startup. Learn more at www.coachingcareprofessionals.com.